SQUADRONS!

No. 19

THE BOULTON PAUL

DEFIANT

DAY AND NIGHT FIGHTER

PHIL H. LISTEMANN

ISBN: 979-1096490-06-6

Copyright

© 2017 Philedition - Phil Listemann

Revised 2018, updated Feb.2020, May 2022

Colour profiles: Juanita Franzi/aeroillustrations

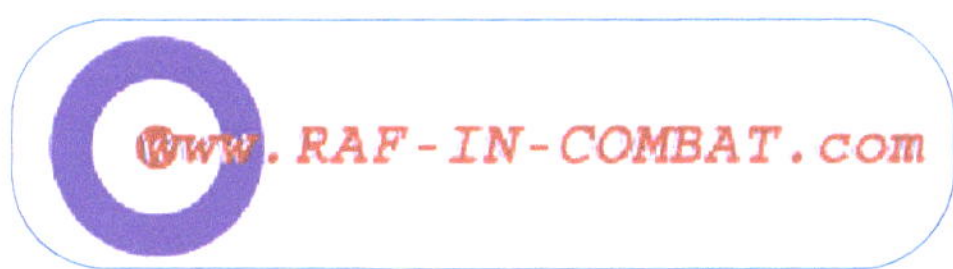

Contributors & Acknowledgments:
André Bar, Jan Joli, Paul Sortehaug, Andrew Thomas

GLOSSARY OF TERMS

PERSONEL :
(AUS)/RAF: Australian serving in the RAF
(BEL)/RAF: Belgian serving in the RAF
(CAN)/RAF: Canadian serving in the RAF
(CZ)/RAF: Czechoslovak serving in the RAF
(NFL)/RAF: Newfoundlander serving in the RAF
(NL)/RAF: Dutch serving in the RAF
(NZ)/RAF: New Zealander serving in the RAF
(POL)/RAF: Pole serving in the RAF
(RHO)/RAF: Rhodesian serving in the RAF
(SA)/RAF: South African serving in the RAF
(US)/RAF - RCAF : American serving in the RAF or RCAF

RANKS
G/C : Group Captain
W/C : Wing Commander
S/L : Squadron Leader
F/L : Flight Lieutenant
F/O : Flying Officer
P/O : Pilot Officer
W/O : Warrant Officer
F/Sgt : Flight Sergeant
Sgt : Sergeant
Cpl : Corporal
LAC : Leading Aircraftman

OTHER
ATA: Air Transport Auxiliary
CO : Commander
DFC : Distinguished Flying Cross
DFM : Distinguished Flying Medal
DSO : Distinguished Service Order
Eva. : Evaded
ORB : Operational Record Book
OTU : Operational Training Unit
PoW : Prisoner of War
PAF: Polish Air Force
RAF : Royal Air Force
RAAF : Royal Australian Air Force
RCAF : Royal Canadian Air Force
RNZAF : Royal New Zealand Air Force
SAAF : South African Air Force
s/d: Shot down
Sqn : Squadron
† : Killed

THE DEFIANT

The RAF's pair of eight-gun monoplane fighters, the Hurricane and Spitfire, that bore the brunt of the desperate fighting over England in the grim summer of 1940, were the product of imaginative foresight and innovative design. The third of Fighter Command's single engine monoplane fighters to see action during the Battle of Britain was, however, the victim of the outdated concept of the two-seat fighter and, as a result, its crews suffered. The Boulton Paul P.82 was a clean, low wing design, later named 'Defiant', powered by a 1,030 hp Rolls-Royce Merlin I engine, the best available British engine at that time. Two prototypes were ordered on 4 December 1935 to meet specification F.9/35 which called for a two-seat turret fighter with a performance approaching that of the new single-seat monoplane fighters being developed to meet specification F.10/35.

The first prototype, K8610, flew from Wolverhampton Airport on 11 August 1937. It was wedded to a neat and compact Boulton Paul power operated turret, but unlike the Hawker Demon biplane it was to replace, the Defiant lacked any forward firing armament, thereby sowing the seeds for its lack of success as a day fighter. The RAF seems to have been very confident in the future of the Defiant as, some months before the first flight of the prototype on 28 April 1937, an order was placed for 87 aircraft under contract No.622849/37 (serials **L6950-L7036**).

The early trials showed promise though, in part, this was because the turret was not installed so the first indications of performance were encouraging. Although some minor problems were encountered, the aircraft proved to be satisfactory enough for a further production order of 202 aircraft, serials **N1535-N1812** (Contract 757867/39), to be placed in January 1938. However, the following month a fully equipped turret was installed which, with the gunner and ammunition, weighed 815 lb (330 kg), almost ten per cent of a fully loaded Defiant!

Intensively tested during 1938, the turret considerably altered the overall performance, but nonetheless an order for 161 more Defiant Mk.Is (**N3306-N3520**) was placed in May that year, making for a total of 450 aircraft. This order was placed according to the production forecasts of Boulton Paul which stated they were expecting to have delivered 450 units by March 1940 at an optimistic production rate of fifty aircraft per month.

The second prototype (K8620) flew for the first time on 18 May 1939 and incorporated changes which were deemed necessary after experience with the first. It was fitted with a Merlin II instead of the troublesome Merlin I. K8620 was also nearer to the production standard Defiant. Soon afterwards, on 30 July 1939 the first production aircraft flew. It differed from the second prototype by being fitted with a new spinner and incorporating some improvements, though the overall performance was little changed. At the outbreak of war in September 1939, only one more Defiant had been delivered to the RAF and by the end of the year the RAF had only fifteen on strength. Despite being behind the delivery schedule, Boulton Paul received another order for a further 150 Defiants in December (**T3911-T4121**) against Contract 34864/39. This contract was amended to add a further fifty aircraft (**V1106-V1183**)

The first Defiant prototype (K8310), seen without its turret, was an elegant design outwardly similar to the Hurricane at first sight.

Side view of the first prototype Defiant turret fighter. Britain was the only country to develop this genre of fighters in what proved to be a flawed concept.

in February 1940 for a total on order of 650. However, despite of the new orders, the Air Ministry remained concerned about the delays and the knock on effect of the type's readiness for operations. By March 1940 only two squadrons were working up when there should have been 450 aircraft on charge.

During the Battle of Britain, and after the first successes of the Defiant over Dunkirk, a final order was placed in July for 300 aircraft (**AA281-AA713**). The first 63 were built as Defiant Mk.Is while the next 203 were built as Defiant Mk.IIs powered with a new version of the Merlin, the XX rated at 1,280 hp. The last thirty of this order (AA687-AA713), and a later order of 300 Mk.IIs (**AV508-AV944**) would be cancelled when the Defiant was found to be obsolete as a night fighter. The last night fighter Defiant, AA670, was taken on charge by the RAF on 15 May 1942. Most of the Mk. IIs would never be issued to any night fighter squadrons and were later used, or converted, for second-line duties like target-towing. Regarding to its contribution to the RAF, the Defiant was credited with 155 victories and flew about 5,200 operational sorties (all but 665 at night).

The Boulton Paul Type A Mk.IID turret with its gunner ready to fire.

Left, K8310, the first prototype with a fully equipped turret. The Defiant was designed to replace the Hawker Demon, but as it was not ready in sufficient numbers, the Demon squadrons were re-equipped with other types. By May 1940, when the Germans launched their offensive, 650 Defiants were on order, but only one squadron was operational.
Below, two prototypes of the Defiant Mk.II flew, N1550 and N1551 (the 103rd and the 104th airframe built respectively). When the various tests were completed, N1551 was stored at No. 46 MU before it was lost in an accident during a ferry flight on 14 February 1943. The main external identifier of a Mk.II, when compared to a Mk.I, was the larger air intake.

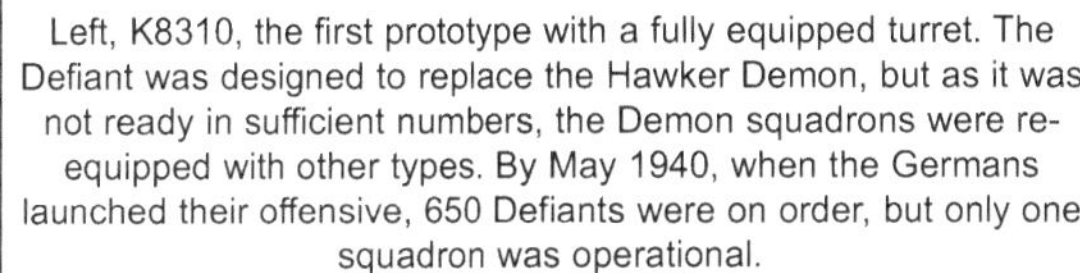

Number of sorties: ca. 700

**First operational sortie:
29.06.40**
**Last operational sortie:
04.08.41**

Number of claims: 15.00

Total aircraft written-off: 13

Aircraft lost on operations: 10
Aircraft lost in accidents: 3

Squadron code letters:
TW

COMMANDING OFFICERS				
S/L William A. Richardson	RAF No. 29047	RAF	...	19.09.41
S/L Edward C. Wolfe	RAF No. 37705	RAF	13.09.40	06.07.41
W/C George F.W. Haycock	RAF No. 26138	RAF	06.07.41	...

SQUADRON USAGE

Number 141 Squadron was the second squadron to receive the Defiant. It had been reformed shortly after the outbreak of war on 4 October 1939 at Turnhouse, near Edinburgh, under the command of S/L W.A. Richardson. It received a miscellany of types for training, using Gladiators and Blenheims for working up at Grangemouth and Prestwick, before converting to the Defiant in April 1940 for which it returned to Turnhouse. Its first Defiant, L6983, arrived on the 4th flown by Pilot Officer Whitehouse of No. 264 Squadron. Unlike 264 Squadron, 141 had a high proportion of Dominion personnel among its crews. Four days later, two Defiants (L6994 and L6995) were taken on charge, but before the end of the month, only one more had arrived (L6984 delivered on the 16th).

The first solos on Defiants were carried out on the 13th, the previous days having been used for ground training. With the few aircraft on hand, training continued for the rest of the month, but by 1 May the squadron was far from operational. The last Gladiators left two days later and the same day five new Defiants arrived. With the opening of the German offensive on 10 May 1940, training, including some by night, was intensified. During one training flight, the squadron suffered its first casualties when, on 15 May, Defiant L6991 crashed near the aerodrome killing Sgt Stephen Keene and AC2 David Wightman.

On 3 June, the squadron was declared operational even though it was short of air gunners. On 14 June, L7012 was severely damaged when P/O Arthur W. Smith, an American-born Canadian, forgot to lower the undercarriage when landing. Fortunately the Defiant was repairable. On 16 June, four commissioned air gunners were posted to the squadron, while night training was increased, and by 23 June five pilots became

When war broke out, Edward Wolfe was already a flight commander with 64 Sqn. In October 1939, he was posted to 219 Sqn flying Blenheims. He would serve there until September 1940 when he joined 141 Sqn as OC. He relinquished command of the squadron when it required a wing commander position upon the introduction of the Beaufighter and was eventually posted to 456 (RAAF) Sqn in March 1942 as CO. He was taken off operational flying in February 1943 until the end of war and was released from the RAF in December 1945 having earned a DFC while serving with 141.

Four of the participants of the disastrous operation of 19 July. Left, Hugh Tamblyn, a Canadian who, with his gunner Sgt Powell, made the first confirmed claim of the squadron while flying a Defiant. Right, the New Zealander, John Gard'ner; below left, John Kemp; and below right, Rudal Kidson, also New Zealanders. The latter two were killed during the engagement. *(Gard'ner, Kemp and Kidson, via Paul Sortehaug)*

operational for night patrols. Five days later, an air raid warning was sounded in the morning and pilots and air gunners stood by at dispersal, but were not scrambled. The following day, the squadron flew its first operational patrols when a section was sent to investigate a raid, but was later ordered to land. The crews were P/O John Waddingham/Sgt Dudley Slatter (L6983), Sergeants Russel Hamer/Ernest Salway (L6988) and George Laurence/Wilfred Chard (L7016).

At the beginning of July, the number of sorties increased and B Flight moved to Prestwick to cover a convoy on the 4th, returning to Turnhouse the following day. On the 8th, P/O A.N. Constantine's Defiant, hit on the ground by an aircraft flown by Pilot Officers R.E. Orchard, a New Zealander, and Francis C.A. Lanning, was written off. It was the second Defiant lost before any contact with the enemy (not including some visual contacts made early in the month). The following day, 141 received orders to move to West Malling in Kent. This was completed on the 12th. The squadron was now in the very heart of the front line against the Luftwaffe as

Photographs of the early days of 141 Sqn are rare. Here Defiant L7000, coded TW-P, is seen during the early stages of the Battle of Britain.

Air gunners of 141 Sqn posing in front of TW-O, circa September 1940. The squadron's brief participation in the Battle of Britain was violent and bloody. (*Andrew Thomas*).

the Battle of Britain moved towards its climax. The squadron's level of activity gradually increased with almost seventy sorties flown up to the 19th, which was to prove a fateful day.

At 1230, 141 was called to patrol south of Folkestone at a height of 5,000 feet. Twenty minutes earlier, air raid sirens had sounded in Folkestone warning that approaching raiders had been detected. Of the twelve Defiants scrambled, only nine, led by S/L Richardson, were actually able to take-off. They were vectored to intercept some Bf110 twin-engine fighters, but had not been warned of Bf109s in the area (III./JG51 led by Hauptmann Hannes Trautloft, a highly experienced veteran of Spain and Battle of France). Flying high, with the sun at his back, Trautloft had no problem spotting the Defiants climbing out and he dived his unit towards them. The Defiant gunners spotted the Bf109s very late and in just a few minutes, six Defiants were shot down, four falling into the sea and two crashing on landing. Of the twelve crewmembers, only two were picked up, P/O Gard'ner, a New Zealander who was injured, and P/O Farnes, F/L Louden's air gunner. Only the aircraft of the CO, S/L Richardson and P/O Halliwell (L6999) and P/O H.N. Tamlyn and Sgt S.W.N. Powell (L7014) returned. A third aircraft (L6983) flown by P/O MacDougall and Sgt Wise, was able to land damaged, but the air gunner had already bailed out over the sea and was never seen again. On this occasion the Germans over-claimed, claiming no less than eleven Defiants as destroyed. Among those that claimed one victory were several notable aces including Trautloft or *Oberleutnant* Arnold Lignitz. *Oberleutnant* Walter Oesau, a future 100-mark pilot, claimed two and three went to *Leutnant* Werner von Pichon-Kalau vom Höfe. In return, 141 Squadron was able to claim its first victory as P/O H.N. Tamblyn and his gunner were able to claim the destruction of a Bf109 while the CO and his gunner claimed a probable. The Germans did lose an aircraft from 9./JG51 which had been badly damaged and crashed on landing. Its pilot, *Feldwebel* Heilmann, died the next day. The pilots of No. 111 Squadron, who had tried in vain to save the Defiants, believed they had seen four Bf109s fall in flames, but they had clearly mistaken the Bf109s for the four Defiants that were shot down in flames! Before the end of the day, the squadron was withdrawn from operations for a short period having suffered a battering in their first action due to the misfortune of encountering a battle hardened German unit in less than ideal conditions.

Over the next few days, seven replacement Defiants arrived and Pilot Officers Tamblyn and Williams became acting flight commanders. On 21 July, the squadron was ordered to move to Prestwick from where patrols were resumed on the 28th.

During August, there were several changes of personnel with Tamblyn, posted to No. 242 (Canadian) Squadron, being replaced by F/L T.B. Fitzgerald, a New Zealander, who had earned the DFC while flying Fairey Battles during the Battle of France. Flight Lieutenant Louden and P/O Gard'ner, who had been injured during the 19 July engagement, returned from hospital. New pilots and air gunners were also posted to the squadron, among them Pilot Officers W.A. Cuddie, a Canadian from Alberta, C.G. Houghton, D.L. Hughes and R.M.McT.D. Lucas. While there was little air activity, 89 sorties were flown during the month including twenty at night (something that would increase in the coming weeks).

Relegated to night fighter duty, the squadron carried out patrols almost every night, but the Luftwaffe was concentrating most of its effort by day. On 13 September, the new CO, S/L Edward C. Wolfe, arrived from No. 219 Squadron. The first night success

John Waddingham made the first night claims of the squadron with his gunner, Sgt Cumbers. Waddingham was killed on 27 September 1942 in Malta while serving with 89 Sqn. Cumbers survived the war. *(J. Gard'ner via P. Sortehaug).*

occurred during the night of 15/16 September when, around midnight, P/O J. Waddingham and his gunner Sgt Cumbers shot down a He111 and claimed another probably destroyed one and a half hours later. They would be awarded the DFC and the DFM respectively a few weeks later for this action. Two nights later, it was the turn of Sgt Chard, with a Defiant piloted by Sgt Laurence, to shoot down a Ju88. During another patrol in L7000 during the night 23/24 September, the crew of Pilot Officers Williams and Pledger sighted an enemy aircraft, but were unable to intercept. With three claims in September in about ninety sorties and no losses, the results can be seen as rather good compared to the previous month. In October, while the Battle of Britain was coming to an end, night patrols continued and 79 were flown, but no further claims were made even though enemy aircraft were sighted on four occasions. Each time the crew was unable to give chase. Another problem also arose as crews were shot at by AAA, fortunately without any major consequences. However on the 30th October, Sergeant G. Laurence crashed N1566 returning from night patrol owing to his instruments being fozen up causing a stall on approach. In November, the squadron moved to Gravesend to protect the South-East London area (the move taking place on the 4th). However, owing to bad weather, some aircraft had to land at another aerodrome and P/O Marsland crashed near Kenley, fortunately without injury to himself or his gunner. Patrols resumed at once and 79 would be carried out during the month, including some over France. On 8/9 and 9/10 November, enemy aircraft were sighted, but not attacked, but luck returned on the evening of the 10th when a Ju88 was attacked by Sergeants Hamer and Hill, the latter firing five bursts from astern. However, the enemy gunner returned fired and damaged the Defiant which had to land immediately. The Ju88 was claimed as a probable. That would be the only claim for the month even though, again, enemy aircraft continued to be sighted (including over France). The 29th was a bad day for the squadron. First, the CO's Defiant collided with another aircraft while taxiing and F/L Fitzgerald had trouble with his undercarriage which eventually collapsed on landing. For each incident the aircraft were extensively damaged. Unfortunately, no further claims were made for the month. Bad weather prevented much operational flying, less than forty night patrols being flown, but despite this, 141 was able to shoot down one He111 near Etchingham (P/O J.G. Benson and P/O Blain) late in the afternoon of the 22nd. The squadron's crews also saw enemy aircraft twice that month, but did not pursue them. On the negative side, Sergeants Laurence and Chard crashed on take-off for a night patrol on 29 December. Laurence was injured and had to be taken to hospital. Little activity was recorded in January, with 25 night patrols flown and encounters rare. However, three enemy aircraft were sighted up to the 17th, but could not be chased down. On the 12th, returning from a patrol, P/O Benson misjudged his approach and his Defiant hit a heap of sandbags, crashed and burst in to flames. Benson and his gunner, P/O Blain, evacuated the aircraft in time, but were taken to the hospital. Operational flying ceased after the 17th until the end of the month owing to bad weather conditions. Operational patrols resumed on 4 February and, as weather progressively improved during the month, the number of sorties increased with close to sixty flown. One enemy aircraft was chased across the Channel on the 16th by F/L Wilson and P/O Pearmain, but they did not catch it. That was the only significant event of the month other than the crash of N1706 on the 26th when returning from a patrol. Owing to bad visibility, F/O Constantine misjudged his landing. Neither him nor his gunner, Sgt Coxon, were injured. March was similar to February in the number of sorties and the loss of one Defiant when N1795 crashed on the 24th following engine failure during a test flight. The crew escaped injury (Flying Officers D.C. Williams and G.F. Pledger). Three patrols were flown on 3/4 April and four on 4/5. Returning

Defiant N1752/TW-L on patrol during the winter of 1940-1941. It was taken on squadron charge in November 1940 and left the following September. *(Andrew Thomas)*

from one patrol that night, Flying Officers Williams and Pledger were killed in a crash (T3913) approximately 2.5 miles from the aerodrome. Their second crash in two weeks had been fatal to both this time. Three days later, P/O Stevens and Sgt Ashcroft claimed a He111 destroyed at 23.50 over Biggin Hill. At the end of the month, the squadron received orders to move to Ayr, south of Glasgow, in Scotland. The move was started on the 29th, the squadron having carried out a final sortie from Gravesend the previous night. This move to Ayr was very fractious and remained incomplete until the 9th. Despite this, night patrols were flown from the 1st. The number of sorties increased and nine sorties were carried out on 5/6 May. One He111 was claimed as destroyed by P/O A.D. Meredith and Sgt Mott after midnight, another by Sergeants George Laurence and Hithersay, and one damaged by F/L Wilson and Sgt Powell. The number of sorties reached its peak with fifteen on 6/7 May during which 141 claimed two confirmed He111s (F/L D.F. Wilson and Sgt Powell) while Pilot Officers Robert L.F. 'Bingo' Day and Francis C.A. Lanning made contact in two sorties with two He111s and one Ju88 and claimed the latter (from 5./KG30) as destroyed and one of the He111s (from 2./KG53) as well. The CO with Sgt Ashcroft sealed the fate of a Ju88 the same night (but the claim was made initially on a He111). During May, the CO was awarded the DFC and Sgt Laurence the DFM while, for their actions during the night 6/7 May, Day and Lanning received the DFC. After that exciting and intense two nights, routine took over and the month ended with no major events to report. In May, the squadron had carried out 87 sorties.

In June, winds of change began to blow when the first Blenheim arrived on the 5th. The Blenheim was the precursor for conversion to the Beaufighter IF. That would be followed ten days later by three other Blenheims and the first Beaufighter was delivered on the 26th while operational flying continued on Defiants. Fifty-eight night patrols were recorded in June with nothing to report. A Beaufighter squadron was required to be commanded by a wing commander, so S/L Wolfe relinquished command on 6 July to the new CO, W/C Haycock. Wolfe stayed on as a squadron leader flying while several of the Defiants and crews were posted to the newly formed No. 410 (RCAF) Squadron formed at Ayr on 30 June 1941. While training continued on Beaufighters, the Defiants were used for operational duties and 58 night patrols were flown in July. This situation lasted until the beginning of August when the last three night patrols were carried out on 4/5 August. The squadron was then stood down to complete the training on the Beaufighters. Operations resumed on 25 August.

Date	Pilot	SN	Origin	Type	Serial	Code	Nb	Cat.
19.07.40	P/O Hugh N. **Tamblyn**	RAF No. 40862	(CAN)/RAF	Bf109	**L7014**		1.0	C
	Sgt Sydney W.M. **Powell**	RAF No. 747702	RAF					
	S/L William A. **Richardson**	RAF No. 29047	RAF	Bf109	**L6999**		1.0	P
	P/O Antony B. **Halliwell**	RAF No. 77354	RAF					
15.09.40	P/O John **Waddingham**	RAF No. 40867	RAF	He111	**N1552**		1.0	C
	Sgt Alfred B. **Cumbers**	RAF No. 746780	RAF					
				He111	**N1552**		1.0	P
17.09.40	Sgt George **Laurence**	RAF No. 518381	RAF	Ju88	**L6988**		1.0	C
	Sgt Wilfred T. **Chard**	RAF No. 746805	RAF					
10.11.40	Sgt Russel C. **Hamer**	RAF No. 566261	RAF	Ju88	**N1622**		1.0	P
	Sgt Charles R. **Hill**	RAF No. 745903	RAF					
22.12.40	P/O James G. **Benson**	RAF No. 81365	RAF	He111	**N1544**		1.0	C
	P/O Leonard M. **Blain**	RAF No. 79228	RAF					
08.04.41	P/O Eldred J. **Stevens**	RAF No. 82660	RAF	He111	**N1800**		1.0	C
	Sgt Alfred E. **Ashcroft**	RAF No. 745591	RAF					
05.05.41	P/O Arthur D. **Meredith**	RAF No. 62651	RAF	He111	**N3430**		1.0	C
	Sgt Walter H. **Mott**	RAF No. 751134	RAF					
	Sgt George **Laurence**	RAF No. 518381	RAF	He111	**T3942**		1.0	C
	Sgt Arthur J.B. **Hithersay**	RAF No. 749366	RAF					
06.05.41	F/L Donald F. **Wilson**	RAF No. 41891	(NZ)/RAF	He111	**N3394**		2.0	C
	Sgt Sydney W.M. **Powell**	RAF No. 747702	RAF					
	P/O Robert L.F. **Day**	RAF No. 41263	RAF	He111	**N1796**		1.0	C
	P/O Francis C.A. **Lanning**	RAF No. 79580	RAF					
				Ju88	**N1796**		1.0	C
	S/L Edward C. **Wolfe**	RAF No. 37705	RAF	Ju88	**T3926**		1.0	C
	Sgt Alfred E. **Ashcroft**	RAF No. 745591	RAF					

Total: 15.00

Sergeant George Laurence, seen in his Defiant, was among the first to make a night claim on 141's account. He was awarded the DFM in May 1941 and was later commissioned. He completed his tour with 141 in December 1941 after having transitioned to the Beaufighter. He was killed during his second tour on 9 November 1944 while serving with 219 Sqn in the Mediterranean.

Date	Pilot	S/N	Origin	Serial	Code	Fate
19.07.40	F/L Ian D.G. **Donald**	RAF No. 33306	RAF	**L7009**	TW-H	†
	P/O Arthur C. **Hamilton**	RAF No. 78543	RAF			†
	P/O John R. **Kemp**	RAF No. 41850	(NZ)/RAF	**L6974**		†
	Sgt Robert **Crombie**	RAF No. 903506	RAF			†
	P/O Richard A. **Howley**	RAF No. 41705	(NFL)/RAF	**L6995**		†
	Sgt Albert G. **Curley**	RAF No. 747968	RAF			†
	P/O Rudal **Kidson**	RAF No. 41297	(NZ)/RAF	**L7015**		†
	Sgt Frederick P.J. **Atkins**	RAF No. 903401	RAF			†
	P/O John R. **Gard'ner**	RAF No. 41841	(NZ)/RAF	**L7016**		-
	P/O Dudley M. **Slatter**	RAF No. 44597	RAF			†
	F/L Malcolm J. **Loudon**	RAF No. 37293	RAF	**L7001**		-
	P/O Eric **Farnes**	RAF No. 77374	RAF			-
30.10.40	Sgt George **Laurence**	RAF No. 518381	RAF	**N1566**		-
	Sgt Wilfred T. **Chard**	RAF No. 746805	RAF			-
29.12.40	Sgt George **Laurence**	RAF No. 518381	RAF	**N1806**		-
	Sgt Wilfred T. **Chard**	RAF No. 746805	RAF			-
12.01.41	P/O James G. **Benson**	RAF No. 81365	RAF	**N1688**		-
	P/O Leonard M. **Blain**	RAF No. 79228	RAF			-
04.04.41	F/O Dennis C. **Williams**	RAF No. 41230	RAF	**T3913**		†
	F/O Geoffrey F.C. **Pledger**	RAF No. 79216	RAF			†

Total: 10

Date	Pilot	S/N	Origin	Serial	Code	Fate
15.05.40	Sgt Steven F.H. **Keene**	RAF No. 514292	RAF	**L6991**		†
	AC2 David **Wightman**	RAF No. 903325	RAF			†
08.07.40	P/O Russel E. **Orchard**	RAF No. 41313	(NZ)/RAF	**L6998**		-
	P/O Francis C.A. **Lanning**	RAF No. 79580	RAF			-
23.03.41	F/O Dennis C. **Williams**	RAF No. 41230	RAF	**T3913**		-
	F/O Geoffrey F.C. **Pledger**	RAF No. 79216	RAF			-

Total: 3

Number of sorties: *ca.* **950**

First operational sortie:
02.02.41
Last operational sortie:
18.04.42

Number of claims: 12.50

Total aircraft written-off: 8

Aircraft lost on operations: 4
Aircraft lost in accidents: 4

Squadron code letters:
DZ

COMMANDING OFFICERS

S/L Jack S. Adams	RAF No. 37728	RAF	...	09.10.41
S/L Ralph I.G. MacDougall	RAF No. 29041	RAF	09.10.41	19.02.42
S/L Irving S. Smith	RAF No. 43048	(NZ)/RAF	19.02.42	...

SQUADRON USAGE

Reformed in 1936 as the RAF began to expand, 151 Squadron started the war as a day fighter unit flying Hurricanes. It participated in the cover of the evacuation of Dunkirk, then fought in the Battle of Britain. With the Luftwaffe switching to night operations, the RAF had a sudden need for night fighters and 151 was officially chosen to operate by night from 20 October 1940 onwards. Commanded by S/L Hamish West from September, the squadron stayed at Digby, near Lincoln, and the initial scheme was to provide one section at readiness every night and one by day with one more available at fifteen minutes. West would be

replaced by S/L Jack C. Adams on 5 December, posted from No. 303 (Polish) Squadron where he was a flight commander, shortly before 151 received its first Defiants on the 12th (N1633, N1636, N1677, N1757, N3317, N3328 and N3337) followed on the 15th by N1539, N1540 and N1738. Ten more followed before the end of December. The squadron then became a huge unit as the number of Hurricanes remained at eighteen for the time being. This number was reduced by a third by the end of the month, the squadron passing five of its Hurricanes to the recently formed No. 71 (Eagle) Squadron. As far as the Defiant was concerned, December was spent in training, while the operational flights were flown on Hurricanes.

Training continued in January while the first night claims were made by the Hurricanes (15/16 January) with two confirmed German bombers and two more probably destroyed. At last the squadron became operational on its Defiants and a first patrol was mounted on 2 February. Sergeant H.G. Bodien and his gunner, Sgt Morris, patrolled in N3387 between 23.45 and 01.25. The patrol was uneventful. Two nights later, two more patrols were flown and Sgt Bodien, teamed this time with Sgt Jonas, intercepted a Do17 at 10,000 feet over Welson at 21.40 and

Jack Adams was already a flight commander with 29 Sqn when war broke out. He served with this unit until the end of August 1940 when he was posted to 303 (Polish) Sqn. In December 1940 he joined 151 Sqn as CO. After he left the squadron, he was rested and completed another tour as OC 256 Sqn and then a third as OC 226 Sqn, a Mitchell unit. Ending the war with a DFC and Bar, he continued to serve in the RAF until August 1958.

Defiant N1791/DZ-K on patrol in 1941. This Defiant was received by the squadron at the end of December 1940 and would serve until September of the following year. Serving with various second line units, it was struck off charge in April 1945. *(Andrew Thomas)*

shot it down in flames after two five second bursts from fifty yards and 25 yards respectively. During the month, the squadron's Defiants flew 33 patrols in all and, while no more claims were added, one Defiant had to be abandoned during a night patrol after running out of petrol. Sadly, the gunner, Sgt Wallace (RNZAF), opened his parachute too early and it caught around the tail and he was dragged to his death. March was rather quiet, but this was hampered by the death of F/O P.L. Gordon-Dean and Sgt G.E. Worledge during a weather test on the 4th. The crash was caused by the loss of a wing during a dive (possibly after a loss of orientation) and if we except the unsuccessful interception of a German bomber by Sergeants Staples and Parkin on the 30th, there was nothing else to report for March. Things changed soon after when the Blitz was re-opened and the German bombers began to appear more often providing further opportunities. On the night of 8/9 April, the squadron claimed four He111s destroyed and one more damaged near Coventry around midnight, the Defiant crews being responsible for two and the damaged Heinkel. A bit later, over Birmingham this time, the Defiant crews added one Ju88, shared with the AA, two He111s destroyed and one Do17 probable. One of the squadron's Hurricanes scored one more the following night (P/O Richard P. Stevens, who would become one of the RAF's night fighter top scorers). In April, the Defiants flew close to ninety night patrols, but this number reduced to seventy in May. There were still some successes, however, with, F/L A.T. Edmiston and Sgt Beale shooting down a Ju88 and Pilot Officer Bodien and Wrampling a He111 within two nights. It was a rewarding time for Bodien as he received his commission on the 4th. On the 7th, S/L Adams intercepted three bombers, but each time was unable to bring his gunner into a good position to open fire. The next night the aerodrome was bombed causing some casualties (but none as far as the Defiants were concerned). The squadron had its revenge two nights later when five claims were made including two by the Defiants - Sergeants Copeland and Sampson sealing the fate of a He111 while F/L McMullen and Sgt Fairweather dispatched another one. Flying Officer Gayzler and Pilot Officer Pfleger (Poles) tried to intercept a Bf110, but the Defiant was too slow. The aerodrome was bombed again that night, but no casualties were reported.

As the Luftwaffe departed for the Eastern Front, the air activity over Great Britain diminished. Ninety-two sorties were flown in June as far as the Defiant was concerned. While P/O Richard Stevens was continuing to increase his score, the Defiants scored only once that month when, at 23.55 on the 21st, P/O G.A.T. Edmiston and his gunner, Sgt Beale, shot down a Ju88 off Cromer. The number of sorties dropped to 39 in July, but no claims were made by the Defiant crews. Sixty-two sorties were flown in August. Alongside the operational duties, crews had a lot to do as, during the month, the squadron was deeply involved in co-operation duties with Douglas Havocs. In September, about sixty sorties were flown by the Defiants and at the end of the month the first Mk. IIs began to be taken on charge (AA408 and AA417 on the 2nd; AA399 and AA403 on the 25th; AA384, AA418, AA421, AA422, AA423, AA424, AA425, AA426, AA427 and AA430 on the 30th). With the arrival of nine more in October, the

When Adams left, he was replaced respectively by W/C Ralph MacDougall (left) and Ian Smith (right).
Ralph MacDougall led 235 Sqn from its formation until May 1940, then participated briefly in the Battle of Britain. After his command with 151 Sqn, MacDougall did not return to operations before war's end. Irving Smith was a New Zealander and had enlisted in the RAF in January 1939. 151 Sqn was his first operational posting and was where he made all his claims (eight confirmed, one probable and four damaged), on Hurricanes, Defiants and Mosquitos. Later in the war, he would take over 487 (NZ) Sqn flying the Mosquito VI. He ended the war with a DFC and Bar and served in the RAF until his retirement in February 1966.

squadron had entirely renewed its Defiant fleet. Operational patrols more than doubled in October compared to September. Just before, 151 welcomed the new CO, W/C MacDougall, on the 8th. Less than twenty sorties were flown in October, but the month ended with a new victory when P/O A.I. Ritchie and his gunner, P/O Sampson, intercepted four Ju88s east of Yarmouth, claiming one shot down and one damaged after a short combat. The squadron flew regularly on operations during November, the Defiant achieving 124 sorties, while practice continued during the day. During one such flight, returning from formation practice on the 12th, AA428 bounced on landing and stalled from fifty feet. The pilot, Sgt H. Godsmark, was killed instantly while his gunner, Sgt Cross, suffered contusions and fractures to both arms. Three days later, P/O A.I. Ritchie and his gunner, Sgt Beale were in action again when they shot down another Ju88 off Yarmouth at dusk. That would be the only claim made that month. However, the same night, Sergeants V.G. Jee and W. Bainbridge were both posted missing from a patrol and it was presumed that they ditched in the North Sea. Also, Sergeant Beale would be awarded the DFM at the end of the month. The squadron lost another Defiant in December when AA429 was posted missing after having taken off at 07.45 for a dawn patrol. It was later discovered that the Defiant had crashed into the sea near a convoy and while the body of the air gunner Sgt Gazzard was recovered, Sgt Mills was never seen again.

January 1942 was quiet with little activity recorded. In February, F/L Irvin S. Smith, a New Zealander serving in the RAF and B flight commander, took over the squadron. On the evening of the 19th, the new CO and his gunner shot down one Do217 and

Defiant N3328/DZ-Z in which F/L Edmiston and Sgt Beale made a claim over a Ju88 on 3 May 1941. This Defiant left in August 1941 and served with various second line units until being destroyed in an accident in October 1942. *(Andrew Thomas)*

damaged a Ju88. These successes were not the only ones as three other Do217s were damaged by Sergeants Macpherson and Tate (Canadians) and Pilot Officers Wain and Lynes (two). This action took place when the Defiants were patrolling off Cromer at the outer swept channel. It was at the end of their patrol, with the convoy sailing below them, when the pilots saw anti-aircraft fire, directed at two Dorniers, coming from one of the ships. Smith gave orders to chase and caught one of them at twenty feet above the sea. A Ju88 immediately got on the tail of the Defiant and Sgt Beale, Smith's gunner, fired at it, spotting some hits. The Junkers disappeared into the cloud. The second of the two Dorniers was damaged by Sgt Tate before it too escaped into cloud. In the meantime, P/O Wain, on the east side of the convoy, noticed AA fire and saw another Do217. He gave chase and his gunner was able to fire at it, noticing strikes before flying away. As with Smith, a German got on his tail too (a Dornier this time). Lynes opened fire and also saw strikes. The pilots were unable to follow their prey as the Defiant was clearly handicapped by a lack of speed. These would the final claims made by the squadron while flying Defiants. In March, the operational activity was negligible, but two Defiants were lost. AA403 was posted missing from a convoy patrol in poor visibility on the 9th and AA394, during a training flight on the 29th, stalled and crashed during unauthorised low flying after formation flying practice. Both crew were killed.

The end of the Defiant was near and the squadron was selected to convert to the new night fighter, the Mosquito NF II. The first arrived on 6 April. Changes were made within the squadron with the movement of personnel as the Defiant was withdrawn. Training commenced at once on the new mount and the last two patrols with Defiants were carried out on the night of the 18th between 20.40 and 22.10. Some Defiants remained with 151 for a little while for secondary duties. The last one left in early July (AA572).

Claims - 151 Squadron (Confirmed and Probable)

Date	Pilot	SN	Origin	Type	Serial	Code	Nb	Cat.
04.02.41	Sgt Henry E. **BODIEN**	RAF No. 566662	RAF	Do17	**N3387**	DZ-E	1.0	C
	Sgt Dudley E.V. **JONAS**	NZ401809	RNZAF					
09.04.41	Sgt Alan D. **WAGNER**	RAF No. 740760	RAF	He111	**N1790**	DZ-P	1.0	C
	Sgt Samuel **SIDENBURG**	RAF No. 1162329	RAF					
	F/L Desmond A.P. **McMULLEN**	RAF No. 40002	RAF	He111	**N3421**		1.0	C
	Sgt Stanley J. **FAIRWEATHER**	RAF No. 1365020	RAF					
10.04.41	F/L Donald F.W. **DARLING**	RAF No. 40368	RAF	Ju88	**N1808**	DZ-D	0.5+	C
	P/O James S. **DAVIDSON**	RAF No. 81393	RAF					
	Sgt Henry E. **BODIEN**	RAF No. 566662	RAF	He111	**N3387**	DZ-E	1.0	C
	Sgt Dudley E.V. **JONAS**	NZ401809	RNZAF					
03.05.41	F/L Guy A.F. **EDMISTON**	RAF No. 84955	RAF	Ju88	**N3328**	DZ-Z	1.0	C
	Sgt Albert G. **BEALE**	RAF No. 755573	RAF					
04.05.41	P/O Henry E. **BODIEN**	RAF No. 45720	RAF	He111	**N3387**	DZ-E	1.0	C
	Sgt Douglas **WRAMPLING**	RAF No. 1375480	RAF					
10.05.41	Sgt Percy **COPELAND**	RAF No. 740491	RAF	He111	**N3317**	DZ-O	1.0	C
	Sgt Richard W. **SAMPSON**	NZ401465	RNZAF					
	F/L Desmond A.P. **McMULLEN**	RAF No. 40002	RAF	He111	**T4050**	DZ-N	1.0	C
	Sgt Stanley J. **FAIRWEATHER**	RAF No. 1365020	RAF					
21.06.41	F/L Guy A.F. **EDMISTON**	RAF No. 84955	RAF	Ju88	**N1790**	DZ-P	1.0	C
	Sgt Albert G. **BEALE**	RAF No. 755573	RAF					
31.10.41	P/O Alexander I. **McRITCHIE**	RAF No. 89763	(AUS)/RAF	Ju88	**AA417***		1.0	C
	Sgt Richard W. **SAMPSON**	NZ401465	RNZAF					
15.11.41	P/O Alexander I. **McRITCHIE**	RAF No. 89763	(AUS)/RAF	Ju88	**AA408***		1.0	C
	Sgt Albert G. **BEALE**	RAF No. 755573	RAF					
19.02.42	S/L Irvin S. **SMITH**	RAF No. 43048	(NZ)/RAF	Do217	**AA469***		1.0	C
	Sgt Albert G. **BEALE**	RAF No. 755573	RAF					

*Mk II
+Shared with AAA

Total: 12.50

Date	Pilot	S/N	Origin	Serial	Code	Fate
23.02.41	Sgt James **Hopewell**	RAF No. 516702	RAF	**N3388**		-
	Sgt Jack F. **Wallace**	NZ401735	RNZAF			†
15.11.41	Sgt Victor G. **Jee**	RAF No. 1163268	RAF	**AA423***	DZ-F	†
	Sgt William **Bainbridge**	RAF No. 1378960	RAF			†
14.12.41	Sgt Anthony I. **Mills**	RAF No. 1160033	RAF	**AA429***		†
	Sgt Royce V. **Gazzard**	RAF No. 744873	RAF			†
04.03.42	Sgt Lawrence H. **Kelley**	RAF No. 917145	RAF	**AA403***		†
	Sgt Albert H. **Phillott**	RAF No. 1379505	RAF			†

** Mk II*

Total: 4

S/L Smith and Sgt Beale, the team responsible for the squadron's last claim on Defiants (19 February 1942). *(Andrew Thomas)*

Summary of the aircraft lost by accident - 151 Squadron

Date	Pilot	S/N	Origin	Serial	Code	Fate
04.03.41	F/O Peter L. **Gordon-Dean**	RAF No. 33436	RAF	**N1794**	DZ-B	†
	Sgt George E. **Worledge**	RAF No. 1376105	RAF			†
19.08.41	*Believed damaged in a ground accident*	-	-	**N3400**	DZ-Q	-
12.11.41	Sgt Howard A. **Godsmark**	RAF No. 1255377	RAF	**AA428***		†
	Sgt Frederick W.S. **Cross**	RAF No. 920444	RAF			-
29.03.42	P/O Herbert W. **Hart**	RAF No. 115127	RAF	**AA384***		†
	Sgt Aldridge J. **Snook**	RAF No. 917338	RAF			†

** Mk II*

Total: 4

Defiant AA436/DZ-V. This aircraft was one of the Mk.IIs that progressivley replaced the Mk.Is from September 1941. The squadron flew half of its sorties with the Mk.II and therefore became the unit that flew the most operations while equipped with the Mk.II. It was also this mark's top scorer with three confirmed victories. The Mk.II arrived too late to have a brilliant career with the RAF.

Number of sorties: ca. 1,400 (all but 485 at night)

First operational sortie:
12.05.40
Last operational sortie:
30.04.42

Number of claims: 102.33

Total aircraft written-off: 38

Aircraft lost on operations: 30
Aircraft lost in accidents: 8

Squadron code letters:
PS

COMMANDING OFFICERS

S/L Stephen H. HARDY	RAF No. 16153	RAF	01.11.39	24.03.40
S/L Philip A. HUNTER	RAF No. 32081	RAF	24.03.40	19.08.40
S/L George D. GARVIN	RAF No. 34237	RAF	19.08.40	23.11.40
S/L Arthur T.D. SANDERS	RAF No. 33095	RAF	23.11.40	16.06.41
S/L Philip J. SANDERS	RAF No. 36057	RAF	23.11.40	18.12.41
S/L Charles A. COOKE	RAF No. 43634	RAF	18.12.41	14.05.42
W/C Hamish M. KERR	RAF No. 27030	RAF	14.05.42	...

SQUADRON USAGE

The first squadron to be equipped with the Defiant was 264 when it reformed at Sutton Bridge, north of Peterborough, Lincolnshire, on 30 October 1939. The following day, S/L Stephen H. Hardy arrived to command the squadron and, five days later, the first newly qualified pilots began to arrive from No. 12 F.T.S. They were Pilot Officers Alexander MacLeod, Anthony M. Dillon (who soon moved on to No. 229 Squadron), Terrence D. Welsh, Harold G. Tipple, Edward H. Whitehouse, Richard W. Stokes and Michael H. Young. The next day, 6 November, Pilot Officers Mitchell, Patrick E.J. Greenhous, Samuel R. Thomas and David Whitley arrived. Before the end of the year they were joined by two other Pilot Officers, Gordon E. Ellis and Eric G. Barwell. Not all the newcomers

Philip Hunter (left) was a brilliant officer and spent part of his career on the staff at RAF College and at Central Flying School. On the right is George Skelton, an Australian from New South Wales, was a former test pilot at Boulton Paul Aircraft who had an in-depth knowledge of the Defiant. Both played a leading part in introducing the aircraft to service.

Defiant L6969 PS-R, seen in the early weeks of 1940, in the early camouflage. It later became F/L George Skelton's mount and was lost on 13 May over the Netherlands.

were inexperienced so, on the 7th, two flight commanders were posted in - F/L William A. Toyne from No. 213 Squadron and F/L Nicholas G. Cooke from No. 611 Squadron. Further pilots arrived by the end of the month to bring the squadron up to strength. The work-up training then began on three Miles Magisters that had been collected on the 8th, but it appears that the pilots were only informed of their future mount on 14 November! The first Defiants, in the shape of L6959, L6960 and L6961, were taken on charge on 9 December, but as deliveries were slow, the squadron had to temporarily fly a miscellany of other aircraft including some Fairey Battles. Sadly, it was during a ferry flight that the squadron's first loss occurred when, on 16 December, P/O H.G. Tipple was killed in N2129. By 31 December 264 had just nine Defiants on charge. Earlier that month, on the 7th, the squadron moved to Martlesham Heath, near Ipswich, alongside the Aeroplane and Armament Experimental Establishment (A&AEE) which greatly assisted in the trials of the Defiant and the unit's development.

In January 1940, training was intensified from Martlesham, while brand new aircraft continued to arrive, though when F/L N.G. Cooke experienced an engine failure on 25 January, fortunately without major damage, the Defiant was grounded pending an investigation by Rolls-Royce. The ban was soon lifted, however, and training resumed. The first night training was conducted on 15 February by F/L W.A. Toyne though, the following day, another incident occurred when P/O S.R. Thomas force-landed at Clapton without damage to the aircraft or himself. Yet another engine failure was recorded on the first day of March, when P/O Gerald H. Hackwood belly-landed L6962 half a mile from the aerodrome. The Merlin engine was still proving troublesome and that day, the first Defiant (L6951) to achieve thirty hours was sent to Boulton Paul for an inspection. This was slightly unusual as this was usually done at the squadron's facilities, however, for the first inspection, Boulton Paul was anxious to ensure that all was well with its aircraft. The squadron was eventually declared operational on 20 March when it signaled HQ 12 Group that two sections of three aircraft were ready for operational duty. Four days later S/L Philip A. Hunter arrived as CO to replace S/L S.H. Hardy who was promoted to wing commander. He later became Aide-de-Camp to the King. On 13 April, F/L George F.A. Skelton was posted in as B Flight commander, replacing F/L W.A. Toyne who left for No. 17 Squadron with whom he was later awarded the DFC. George Skelton was an important addition to the unit as he was a former Boulton Paul test pilot and had extensive knowledge of the

Defiant L6969 /PS-B, flown by F/L Skelton, lying on the Done river after it had been shot down on 13 May 1940. Skelton became a PoW, but his gunner, J.E. Hatfield, managed to escape.
(Jan Jolie)

Wreckage of L6977/PS-U, also lost on 13 May, being taken away to be scrapped for the German war industry.
(Jan Jolie)

Defiant. Soon afterwards, on 23 April, the first Defiant was wrecked when it caught fire in the air, forcing P/O Greenhous to make an emergency landing near Orfordness. L6952 was a total write-off, but fortunately there were no major injuries to the crew.

During the first months of 1940, 264 worked closely with the Air Fighting Development Unit (AFDU) to establish the best tactics to attack bombers. The CO, Philip Hunter, played an important role in this development and was a key figure in this part of the Defiant story. Thus, by the end of April, three tactics had been adopted: overtaking on a parallel course and firing at the fuselage; converging on a beam attack; and diving across the front of a bomber formation. While the first priority for the Defiant was the bombers, crews also had to be prepared to fight against any enemy fighters providing escort. Some practice flights were carried out against single-seat RAF fighters and the various scenarios flown showed that the Defiant could be an aggressive opponent able to defend itself, the four gun turret being a deadly weapon in the right hands. As ever, success depended on the skill of the pilot. The

Defiant pilots and gunners after their day of greatest success over Dunkirk.
Back row: Pilot Officer G.L. Hickman, Flight Lieutenant N.G. Cooke, Squadron Leader P.A. Hunter, Pilot Officer M.H. Young, Pilot Officers G.H. Hackwood, E.G. Barwell, S.R. Thomas and D. Whitley.
Front row: Sergeant E.R. Thorn, Pilot Officer D.H.S. Kay, Sergeant A.J. Lauder and Pilot Officer R.W. Stokes.

main squadron defensive tactic adopted in the face of fighter attack was a defensive circle that was believed at the time to be robust enough to counter the threat from the Luftwaffe's Bf109s.

With the opening of the German offensive on 10 May, the squadron moved south to Duxford. At that time, the RAF had 58 Defiants on hand, though not all were combat ready. The first sortie by a Defiant was actually carried out at 0100 by F/L Skelton, with P/O Hatfield as gunner, but no contact was made and they landed after an hour. The following day the squadron kept one section at readiness from 0430 and later a convoy patrol was carried out near the Happisburgh Lightship by Red section (comprising S/L Hunter/LAC King and P/O Young/LAC Johnson). They returned after dark with nothing to report. In the early afternoon of the 12th, 'A' Flight, having refueled at Horsham St Faith near Norwich, patrolled The Hague with the Spitfires of No. 66 Squadron. The Defiants took off at 1310 with S/L Hunter and LAC King leading Red Section in L6973. The other Red Section crews were P/O Whitehouse/Sgt Smalley (L6972) and P/O Young/LAC Johnson (L7003) while Yellow Section was led by F/L N.G. Cooke/Cpl A. Lippett (L6975) and P/O Barwell/Sgt Quinney (L6964). The third aircraft of Yellow Section (P/O Whitley/LAC Turner in L6970) had to return early shortly after take-off. The patrol commenced over The Hague at 1355, each section following a section of Spitfires. Five minutes later, off the Dutch coast, they spotted a Ju88 approaching and dropping a bomb near some destroyers. Red Section cut it off as it turned inland and dived to ground level. An overtaking attack was commenced and each aircraft made a cross over attack in turn with the Defiant gunners' tracer fire seen hitting the bomber. Smoke poured from its port engine and the Defiant's first victim crashed in the middle of a field full of cows and surrounded by dykes. The Ju88 was from 5./KG30 and two of the crew were killed with a third dying of wounds a few days later. The fourth was captured. The victory was jointly credited to the three crews of Red Section. Meanwhile, Yellow Section claimed a He111 that was spotted flying at 3,000 feet. While three Spitfires attacked the German bomber from behind, Yellow 1 (L6975) carried out a crossover attack from starboard, at a distance estimated of 100 yards, and the gunner fired 400-500 rounds in two bursts. Soon smoke was noted issuing from both engines. Yellow 2 was in a position to also make a crossover attack from the port side before the aircraft crashed in a field.

The following morning started like the day before when 264's crews saw a number of Ju87s of 12.(St)/LG1 and attacked. The Stukas were not alone, however, as they were escorted by Bf109s of 5./JG26. These immediately attacked the Defiants and five of the six aircraft that had taken off were lost. The Flight of No. 66 Squadron, which was escorting the Defiants, could do nothing to save them. The first to be shot down was L6958, its pilot, P/O S.R. Thomas bailing out, but the gunner, LAC J.S. Bromley, was posted missing. It was followed by L6969 flown by F/L Skelton who made a belly-landing on the banks of the Donge. He was badly wounded and taken to St. Teresa Hospital at Raamsdonksveer where he was later captured. His air gunner, P/O J.E. Hatfield, although wounded, was able to make his way back to the UK the following day. He reported that he was fired at when descending by parachute. He was accompanied by P/O Thomas though both had initially been arrested by the Dutch who mistook them as Germans. L6960 (P/O G.E. Chandler and LAC D.L. McLeish) exploded in mid-air leaving no chance for the crew while the last two Defiants were able to make an emergency landing. The crew of L6977 (P/O E.J. Greenhouse and Sgt F.D. Greenhalgh) was captured, but the crew of L6965 (P/O A. MacLeod and LAC W.E. Cox) was able to return to England and was back with the Squadron on the 17th (after disguising themselves in civilian clothes and catching a ride on a Royal Navy destroyer). The last Defiant, L6974, flown by P/O H.S. Kay and LAC E.J. Jones, made the trip back, but was badly damaged (later repaired). In return however, the

The air gunners of 264 Sqn, who flew during the Defiant's historic action on 29 May 1940, pose for posterity. Among the most successful are, back row: Cpl A. Lippet (first from left), LAC Barker (third from left), LAC S.B. Johnson (fourth from left). Seated in the front row: Pilot Officer C.E. Williams (fourth from left). The only pilot in this photograph is Sergeant R.A. Thorn (first from left).

After the furious combats of May 1940, 264 Sqn continued its training for the inevitable Battle of Britain. Nevertheless, July 1940 was quiet. In this photo, we can see N1536/PS-R, L7026/PS-V and L6967/PS-P.

Defiants claimed four Stukas and one Bf109 destroyed. There was considerable over-claiming by both sides as the Germans claimed no less than eight fighters as destroyed. Only one Defiant was identified as such, the other claims being identified as Spitfires. Only one of 66 Squadron's Spitfires was lost, crashing on landing after having sustained heavy damage.

Despite the congratulatory messages from Boulton Paul Aircraft Ltd and AVM T. Leigh Mallory, AOC 12 Group, the squadron had been shaken up and no flights were made during the following days with only local night patrols being flown on 20 and 21 May. Two days later, the squadron moved to Manston from where patrols over the Dunkirk - Calais - Boulogne area were carried out by a dozen Defiants led by S/L Hunter. The following afternoon, the squadron repeated the same duty, but this time luck was with the Defiant crews. The new B Flight commander F/L E.H. Whitehouse, with P/O H. Cook, in L6972, claimed a Bf110 as destroyed, probably a reconnaissance aircraft as one belonging to 1./Aufkl.Gr.Ob.d.L was lost that day. On the following two days, the squadron carried out numerous patrols in the area of Dunkirk, where fighter cover was needed to cover the start of Operation Dynamo, the evacuation of the British Expeditionary Force from the Continent. It was on the second patrol, 27 May, that the squadron added some more enemy aircraft to its tally when they met some He111s from KG51 shortly after midday. In the ensuing battle three bombers were claimed destroyed and two more 'probable'. In fact, the Germans did lose a Heinkel near Dunkirk with two more returning damaged. The next day was another successful one. In the same area, the Defiants, once more led by the CO, encountered 27 Bf109s. In the ensuing engagement, the Defiants were able to claim six German fighters as destroyed, but three of their own were lost in return. The first to be shot down was L6959 (F/L E.H. Whitehouse and P/O H. Scott) and was quickly followed by L7007 (P/O A. MacLeod and P/O J.E. Hatfield) and L6953 (Sgt L.C.W. Daisley/LAC H. Revill). None of the crews survived. Two of the Defiants were claimed by Oberleutnant Josef 'Pips' Priller, Staffelkapitän of 6./JG51. The squadron mounted a further patrol in the afternoon with nine Defiants, once more led by Hunter, though without result due to poor weather conditions. The Defiant's 'day of fame' came on 29 May. Once again, it all started with patrols carried out around Dunkirk-Calais in conjunction with the Hurricanes of Nos. 56, 151 and 213 Squadrons. The first target for the Defiants remained the bombers and they were detailed to look for them. One Hurricane squadron remained with the Defiants as cover while the two others went for the fighter escort. The Defiants were promptly attacked by six Bf109s which may have mistaken them for Hurricanes and LAC King, the CO's gunner, opened fire at short range setting a Bf109 on fire. King's shooting was followed by that of LAC Hayden, P/O Welsh's gunner, and that Bf109 too was badly hit and broke away. Flight Lieutenant Cooke, with Cpl Lippett, and P/O Young, with LAC Johnson, also each claimed a Bf109 shot down in flames. However, Defiant L6957, flown by P/O Kay and LAC Jones, was hit in the tail during the attack, and the gunner decided to bail out. His body was later found on a French beach. Kay was able to coax his damaged aircraft back. The day was not over, however. Soon after this action, Sgt Thorn and his gunner, LAC Barker, saw an isolated Ju87 and broke away to attack. The crew of the Stuka did not see them coming and in a single burst it was set on fire. Thorn rejoined the rest of the squadron to attack the other Stukas, but the escorting Bf110s dived to protect their charges. In the ensuing dogfight, no less than six Bf110s were claimed (two falling to P/O Stokes and Sgt Fairbrother) while three more Bf109s were also claimed. The German fighters had succeeded in protecting the Ju87s.

Back at Manston, 264 flew a further op later in the day (including P/O Kay flying L6961 with a new gunner, LAC Cox) and were once again protected by a squadron of Hurricanes. Arriving in the area, the Defiants eventually saw a large formation of Ju87s and they made an approach and attacked the Stukas one after the other. At the end of the attack, no less than ten Ju87s were claimed destroyed, five of them to F/L N. Cooke and Cpl A. Lippett alone! With the three Bf109s claimed earlier, this crew had claimed eight German aircraft in an afternoon. Although there was an inevitable duplication of claims made in good faith, these actions gave a boost to the morale. The courage of the Defiant crews cannot be denied and a number of gallantry awards were made to the squadron. Squadron Leader Philip Hunter received a DSO and an immediate DFC went to F/L Cooke. The gunners and non-commissioned pilots were not forgotten as three DFMs were awarded to Corporal Lippett, LAC Barker and King, with another DFM going to Sgt Thorn, a pilot. The next day, the squadron returned to Duxford and was released for the day.

On 31 May, 264 was back over Dunkirk with No. 213 Squadron's Hurricanes and met a large formation of Bf109s and He111s. The German fighters, belonging to III./JG26, attacked first, and the Defiants moved into their defensive circle, but this did not prevent L6968 from being shot down. Pilot Officer G.L. Hickman and LAC A. Fidler were killed. Unfortunately, during this action, L6980 and L6961 collided, though P/O Whitley and LAC Turner, in L6961, were able to crash-land on a beach. L6980 disintegrated and while P/O M.H. Young baled out unhurt, Sgt S.B. Johnston was lost. During this engagement, the squadron was able to claim four Bf109s shot down, and 213 Squadron claimed six more though they lost five Hurricanes to the Bf109s. The Germans did lose three Bf109s with their pilots killed, but claimed nine Hurricanes including two for Leutnant Joachim Müncheberg, a future 'centurion' ace. Later in the day, 264 was airborne again and encountered He111s of KG27. Attacking immediately, they claimed five destroyed. However, the return fire from the German gunners shot down two Defiants - L6975 (F/L N.G. Cooke and Cpl A. Lippett, who were killed), and L6972 (P/O E.G. Barwell and P/O J.E.M. Williams). The latter had a glycol leak and their engine seized about five miles from the English coast forcing them to ditch into the Channel between two destroyers that ultimately rescued them. After this last day of intensive combat, the squadron's pilots were able to evaluate some of the lessons. Among these was that the Germans sometimes mistook the Defiants for Hurricanes. More importantly was the lack of co-operation when flying together with other RAF squadrons as they were often not using the same radio frequency. Nonetheless, the squadron had achieved some considerable successes over Dunkirk with only moderate losses. Squadron Leader Hunter's unit approached the coming Battle of Britain with confidence in both their aircraft and the tactics they had developed.

On the first day of June, P/O Whitley and his gunner, LAC Turner, returned to the squadron and 264 re-established itself at Duxford where it received replacement aircraft and no less than thirteen New Zealand air gunners. The squadron then flew a mix of night patrols and convoy escorts, often mounting these from Martlesham Heath, though air activity remained quiet during the month. On the 4th, F/L Trumble was posted to the squadron to take command of B Flight and, a few days later, Defiant L7004 was lost during a training flight when it was abandoned by its crew (P/O Carnaby and P/O Ellery) after an engine failure. The crew of L6970 was less fortunate a few days later when, on the 11th, during an air firing practice, the aircraft crashed killing P/O Hutcheson and injuring the air gunner LAC Robinson. Once again, the reliability of the Merlin engine was suspected.

At the beginning of July, as Luftwaffe activity over the Channel began to increase, 264 moved to Duxford's satellite at Fowlmere.

Squadron Leader Hunter in PS-A leading a patrol for the camera during July 1940. At that time the RAF was still confident in the capabilities of the Defiant and propaganda photos were happily issued to the Press.

Led by the CO, the charismatic S/L Philip Hunter, two sections of 264 Sqn patrol over England during the Battle of Britain.

Its first action of the Battle of Britain took place on 3 July when eight aircraft of A Flight, led by the CO, took off for an interception, but did not encounter the enemy. During the early days of July new pilots and gunners continued to arrive as air activity increased significantly, but the squadron had no contact with the Luftwaffe during the month.

In August, after the withdrawal of No. 141 Squadron following its mauling, 264 continued flying convoy patrols off the east coast with no sign of action. It was a particular irony that, when the bombers of Luftflotte 5 ventured unescorted across the North Sea to attack targets in Yorkshire, eleven of the squadron's Defiants were on a convoy escort nearby. However, they were ordered to remain with the convoy while the raid was engaged by Spitfires, thus depriving Hunter's turret fighters of a glorious chance to show their worth in their designed role of 'bomber destroyers'. There was, however, already a pointer to the future, as on the night of 15 August, P/O Whitley and Sgt Turner intercepted a Heinkel He111 during a night patrol. The Defiant was spotted when closing to attack and the Heinkel opened fire, but two accurate bursts were fired into the bomber before it escaped into cloud. This was the squadron's first engagement at night and its operational record book states that the Heinkel was: 'later confirmed as destroyed.' On returning from the successful patrol, the gunner reported that the tracer was blinding and between bursts only the pilot was able to see the enemy. It was then suggested that only ball and armour piercing ammunition should be used at night. On 19 August, Squadron Leader G.D. Garvin who had been with the squadron as supernumerary Squadron Leader, took over the squadron, but Hunter, at his own request stayed with the 264 on attachement (he was officially posted to the Air Staff). The next day, 20 August, F/L Campbell-Colqhoun assumed command of B Flight. Meanwhile, in the south, enemy air attacks increased in intensity and despite 141's debacle, the experienced 264 Squadron was recalled into the cauldron of No.11 Group on the 22nd. It was based at Hornchurch, but used Manston as its forward base once again. Red Section had already patrolled Manston in the afternoon and was there again in the evening. Patrols over the Thames Estuary on the 23rd also proved uneventful, but on August 24 the quadron left Hornchurch at 0510 and Red, Yellow and Green sections landed at Manston to refuel before holding at readiness. Blue Section remained above as cover before landing themselves. During the refueling, the squadron was scrambled again, but was recalled after 25 minutes. Then, at 0830, it was ordered to patrol over Manston, however, F/L Campbell-Colquhoun in L7013/PS-U had difficulty starting his engine and was late taking off. Visibility was not very good and he sighted two aircraft that he took to be his section, but they were Bf109s (though identified as He113s) which immediately attacked, hitting the Defiant behind the turret with an explosive shell that ignited Very cartridges. Campbell-Colquhoun took evasive action and returned to Manston without further damage. Other fighters dived upon the squadron, but thanks to effective defensive tactics caused no damage. The Defiants returned to Hornchurch at 1130, but was then ordered to patrol Manston once more. Seven aircraft of A Flight and five from B Flight took off and, after an hour, landed to refuel at Manston. Almost immediately, they were scrambled once again as the airfield came under attack from twenty Ju88s escorted by Bf109s. As there was no time to join up, a squadron attack was impossible, so a series of individual combats developed. Squadron Leader Garvin, P/O Whitley and Sgt Thorn each destroyed a Ju88 and another was damaged by P/O Knocker, while P/O Eric Barwell shot down a Bf109 which was again identified as a He113. However, three Defiants failed to return including S/L Hunter and his gunner P/O King who were last seen by Red Section chasing a Ju88 towards France. The loss of the able Hunter was a severe loss to both the squadron and to Fighter Command. At 1540 the squadron was ordered up again as another raid approached Hornchurch from the south-east. Only seven got into the air as two collided on the ground. In any case, the alert to scramble was given late as bombs were actually exploding on the airfield as the last pair took off! The large formation of Ju88s and He111s, escorted by Bf109s, was at 12,000 feet and once more it proved impossible for the Defiants to get into a proper formation for mutual defence. They found the enemy north-east of Hornchurch with S/L Garvin hitting the main formation and claiming two Ju88s with overtaking and converging attacks. Pilot Officer Welsh attacked a straggler some 400 yards behind the main formation and shot it down in a crossover attack. He also damaged a Bf109. Pilot Officer Young, having become separated

Three unidentified pilots of 264 Sqn chatting at dispersal during the Battle of Britain. Behind is Defiant PS-O (believed to be L7018).
(*via Paul Sortehaug*)

Two photos of 264's Defiants ready for action during the summer of 1940. Above, PS-L is something of a mystery. It appears to be L6996 (the last two digits of the serial being 96) that was apparently lost on 24 August 1940, but there is no trace of this loss that day (see tables). The aircraft flew on the second patrol of the day with N1535 and L6985, but its crew took another aircraft (L7021) for the following patrol and they (Pilot Officer David Whitley/Sergeant Robert Turner) claimed an enemy aircraft destroyed. Even if it is not recorded correctly in the ORB, it is possible that the aircraft was badly damaged returning from patrol and was struck off charge as it disappeared from the squadron's inventory after that date. Below, Defiant L7021/PS-H (also seen in the background of the photo above).
(*Andrew Thomas*)

Defiant L7005/PS-X being prepared for another patrol in August 1940. In the background is L7026/PS-V while, on the right, L7013/PS-U is also receiving attention from the fitters. Below, Defiant L7025/PS-Z being refuelled. It was lost on 26 August 1940 when shot down by Bf109s. Note in the four photos on these two pages that the style of the fuselage roundels varies.

from the main formation, found a solitary He111 that he destroyed in an overtaking attack. Pilot Officer Gaskell was shot down and injured by a Bf109, but his gunner, Sgt Machin, died of wounds.

The following day seven replacement aircraft were delivered to Hornchurch, but, much to the chagrin of the squadron's engineers, many modifications and 48 hours were required to make them operational. Some had no self-sealing fuel tanks, guns required harmonisation and the work during the night was seriously hampered by air raids during which no light was allowed in the hangars. That evening ten aircraft patrolled Dover uneventfully. Late the following morning, 26 August, 264 Squadron, led by F/L Banham, was ordered to intercept an enemy bomber formation approaching Dover. Twelve Do17s, in vic line astern and heavily escorted by Bf 109s, were intercepted at 12,000 feet between Herne Bay and Deal. The Defiants immediately attacked from below, but were in turn attacked by a swarm of Bf109s. Banham brought down a Dornier, but was then hit and set on fire. He rolled on his back calling for his gunner to bail out before jumping himself. He was picked up after one and a half hours in the sea. Sergeant Baker, the gunner, was lost. Pilot Officer Goodall beat off a Bf109 before making an overtaking attack on a Do 17 which caught fire, while future high scoring night fighter ace P/O Desmond Hughes, in his first fight, destroyed two Do17s by converging attacks. Sgt Roland Thorn, soon to be the RAF's leading Defiant pilot with 12½ victories, and Sgt Fred Barker also claimed two of the Dorniers, but when attacking a third they were hit by an escorting Messerschmitt, sustaining oil and glycol leaks. Taking evasive action, Thorn spun away and, as he prepared for a crash landing near Herne Bay, was attacked again at only 500 feet. Although the Defiant caught fire, before crashing, Barker fired his remaining rounds at the enemy fighter which crashed nearby. Both Thorn and Barker escaped with minor injuries and were awarded Bars to their DFMs for their gallantry. Elsewhere, F/O Stephenson was set on fire by a Bf109 and bailed out. He too was picked up in the sea and later taken to Canterbury hospital with minor injuries, but his gunner, Sgt Maxwell, was lost. The squadron claimed seven enemy aircraft destroyed during the fight.

The next afternoon, 264 moved over to Rochford (now Southend Airport) and from there, early the following morning, twelve of its Defiants were ordered to patrol over Dover at 12,000 feet. Near Folkestone, they found twenty He111s with a heavy escort, but as they attacked, they were bounced by the Bf109s of JG26, led by Major Adolf Galland, and split up, so losing the benefits of mutual protection. One of the Heinkels was claimed by P/O Carnaby in his first engagement and another was damaged by Sgt Lauder. Squadron Leader George Garvin in L7021/PS-H had a fuse blow in the turret and, while F/L Ash was replacing it, the aircraft was hit by cannon shells and caught fire. Both bailed out, but Ash was dead when he was found. Worse followed as P/O Whitley and Sgt Turner, one of the most successful crews in the squadron, were killed when their Defiant crashed and burst into flames. Pilot Officers Kenner and Johnson also went down. Pilot Officer Bailey, having claimed the first of his six victories and his only one on the Defiant, also made a forced landing after being hit by a Bf109. Of the eight Defiants that returned, only three were serviceable. On the other side, Major Adolf Galland and Hauptmann Gerhard Schöpfel, had claimed their 26th and 14th victories respectively when they downed a Defiant each, while three more Defiants were claimed by other pilots of JG26. Soon after the squadron's aircraft had been refueled, a large enemy formation was reported approaching Rochford and permission requested for the three avail-

Issued to the squadron in December 1940, Defiant N1801 was mainly flown by F/O Hughes teamed with Sgt Gash *(Andrew Thomas)*

A Defiant of 264 Sqn, coded PS-Z, passing in front of PS-T, taxiing out during the winter of 1940-1941 for another night patrol.
(L.P. Russel via Paul Sortehaug)

able aircraft to take-off. However, this was refused, and, almost as a final insult, the enemy aircraft then bombed the airfield! That afternoon, a chastened 264 Squadron returned to Hornchurch and at 1800 was ordered to return to Kirton in Lindsey the following day. While the squadron detailed three Defiants for convoy escort on the afternoon of 3 September, daytime operations for the Defiant were actually over. Until the end of the month, 264 switched to night patrols and about 100 of them were flown, but not without incident. On the 4th, heading out for a night patrol, N1628 struck the ground after take-off from Kirton in Lindsey. The two crewmembers were killed in the crash. No enemy aircraft was engaged during the month. October saw less air activity, with about sixty patrols flown, and two Defiants were lost. The first, N1578, crashed on the 7th while taking off from Luton for a training flight (B Flight had been there since the beginning of the month) and was followed the next day by N1627. While the crew of the former extracted themselves from the wreckage, injured but safe, the crew of the latter was killed. In October too, no enemy aircraft were engaged. At the end of the month the squadron moved to Southend. After two months of frustration, satisfaction returned when a He111 was claimed as damaged, late in the evening of 23 November, by F/O F.D. Hughes eight miles east of Southend. The same day, a new CO took over the squadron. A pre-war squadron leader, this was the first operational wartime command for S/L Arthur T.D. Sanders. However, misfortune continued in November, with the squadron mourning the loss of N1547 and its crew when it hit trees on approach to Rochford and exploded. Pilot Officer Knocker was killed in the crash, while the gunner, Sgt Tooms, succumbed to his burns soon after. Five days later, it was the turn of N1627 to crash, during take-off this time, but with the same result as the crew were killed. At the end of November, another move took place to Debden, north of London. That did not change anything regarding claims, as none were filed in December, even though the number of sorties was maintained at around 100. On the other hand, and since May 1940, no Defiant was lost in December. The squadron moved once more, to Gravesend, on the 31st.

In January, few sorties were carried out (from Biggin Hill from the 11th). The poor weather was the main cause. However, that was enough to make some interceptions and, on the 9th, one Ju88 was damaged over Beachy Head by Sergeants Hendersby and Chandler. In February, the month was free of any encounters despite flying about ninety sorties. The squadron flew about the same number of sorties in March, but better results were achieved. On the night of 12/13 March, the Luftwaffe once again intensified its raids over the British cities and the Fighter Command night fighter squadrons made various claims against the German bombers. As far as 264 was concerned, two He111s were shot down, followed by one more probable the next night. That claimed was later changed to damaged (Sgt Wilkin/Sgt Crook). On the negative side, a few days previously, two Defiants (N3332 and N3478) had collided during night patrols. Both managed to crash-land and, fortunately, none of the men were killed, but all of them were taken to hospital. Defiant N3332 would be repaired while N3478 was struck off charge later on. At the end of the month, F/Sgt Thorn, who had received the DFM for his actions over Dunkirk, went to Buckingham Palace to receive the Bar to his DFM announced in February (Sgt Barker, his gunner, received the DFM at the same time). The Luftwaffe continued its raids in April (264 moved to West Malling on the 14th) and the harvest continued. The squadron claimed, in the last hours of the 8th, one He111 destroyed by the CO and his gunner, while another was claimed as a probable (F/O Hughes/Sgt Gash). The next night, F/Sgt Thorn and Sgt Barker claimed a He111 as destroyed five minutes before midnight. This was Thorn's last claim of the war. Their thirteen confirmed victories (one shared) made them the leading Defiant crew of the war. One night later, F/O Barwell and Sgt Martin claimed one Ju88 destroyed followed by a probable He111 later in the night during a second patrol. In the early hours of 11th, F/O Hughes and Sgt Gash claimed a He111 destroyed. The squadron continued to fly night patrols until the end of the month, but no more claims were added to the tally. However, one Defiant was lost when, with the radio-transmitter unserviceable, the crew of N3369 became lost and, after running out of fuel, both decided to abandon the Defiant to live to fight another day. Before leaving for the future Eastern Front,

Six Boulton Paul Defiant Mark I night fighters of 264 Sqn, based at West Malling, Kent, flying in port echelon formation.
Below, N3366/PS-B flying in formation.

Defiant N3313/PS-P was usually flown by F/L Thomas and Sgt Shepherd during the summer of 1941. This aircraft would be handed to 456 Sqn in September.

the Luftwaffe wanted to mark its presence and intensified the raids in May and, logically, the number of successes for 264 increased too. In the early hours of the 8th, P/O Curtice, with P/O Martin as gunner, claimed one He111 destroyed and one more damaged over Lille in France during an intruder mission, one of the very few flown by the Defiant. Meanwhile, P/O Grey and his gunner claimed one He111 and two others damaged over the same area. One night later, F/O Young and Sgt Russell, carrying out an intruder mission over Normandy area, shot down a Bf110 and then, two nights later, it was the turn of the CO to score (one He111 destroyed) as well as F/L Stephenson and F/O Magg (one He111 destroyed) and Pilot Officers Curtice and Martin (Do17), the latter during another intruder mission. That would be the last main bomber raid on the British cities until the first month of 1944 when the 'Little Blitz' was launched. The Luftwaffe now had other targets in sight and left British skies by night in relative quietness. Anyhow, this had been a very fruitful month with less than 100 sorties flown and no losses to be reported. In June, bad weather ruined the period of the moon, but, despite this, more than 100, ultimately uneventful, sorties were flown. The new OC from the middle of the month, was another Sanders (P.J) who replaced the current Sanders (A.T.D.). Philip James Sanders was a Battle of Britain veteran who had fought with 92 Squadron. With the main Luftwaffe units now engaged against the Soviet Union, the RAF couldn't help but notice the lack of activity despite the good weather prevailing during the summer. Such a low level of activity hadn't occurred for about a year! The squadron had little to do and only eighty sorties were flown in July, but to compensate, intensive training was carried out. In August, it was worse with the low number of sorties (50) being amplified by the rather bad weather. As for July, the squadron's main occupation became the training flights, one of them ending badly. On the 31st, the pilot of N3453, F/O W.R.A. Knocker, lost control during a searchlight co-operation exercise. The crew bailed out and, even though both suffered leg fractures, they survived. Flight Sergeant Hardy, the gunner, was very fortunate as he jumped out at only 800 feet and his parachute opened just in time! In September, the squadron was busy curing teething problems with the Defiant Mk.II which had begun to arrive at the squadron. The first Mk.IIs taken on charge were AA371, AA373, AA377, AA410 and AA411 between 28 August and 2 September. Others would follow during September. On 7 September, one Defiant was lost after engine failure in flight while training. The crew bailed out and the gunner, Sgt L. Tokarczyk, was injured. In October, the Defiant Mk.II finally gave satisfaction, but the squadron was still facing a total lack of activity. That month, in about sixty sorties, only one encounter was made. Pilot Officer Gray giving chase to a Do217 which later crash-landed, but was not fired at. November and December were similar to the previous months with the only major event taking place on 18 December when S/L Charles A. Cooke from 96 Squadron arrived to assume command. An experienced pilot, he had fought with 66 Squadron during the Battle of Britain.

January 1942 produced little in the way of enemy activity due to a long period of bad weather. Only nine nights were considered flyable and resulted in a total of 28 sorties for the month. February was similar as, in the first nine days, flying was possible on only one occasion. Furthermore, snow, frost and fog made the station unserviceable except in an emergency. That explains why only seventeen patrols were carried out that month. The weather improved greatly in March and more patrols were flown - forty - but no

An interesting inside view of the turret of the Defiant, with Sgt Leslie P. Russell seated inside. Russell was a New Zealander who joined 264 as an air gunner in June 1940, but only completed his training at the end of July. He was teamed with P/O M.H. Young and both claimed, in order, a Ju88 damaged and a He111 and Bf110 destroyed during their association. When 264 gave up its Defiants, Russell was sent to 35 Sqn as a Halifax gunner. He was lost with his aircraft (W1101) during a raid over Mannheim on 19/20 May 1942.
(*L.P. Russel via Paul Sortehaug*)

interceptions made. Normal activity resumed in April, however, with over eighty patrols flown that month. Pilot Officer Watkins chased a Ju88 on the evening of the 2nd, while the Luftwaffe was bombing Dover, but was out-distanced. Three nights later, it was the turn of F/O Clive's air gunner to make visual contact with an enemy aircraft that soon entered cloud and disappeared. At last, 264 made its final claim with the Defiant when P/O A.I. Stuart (RAAF) and his air gunner, F/O M.H. Magg, shot down an He111 south of Beachy Head. This brought the squadron's tally to 97 enemy aircraft destroyed, including fifteen at night. A couple of days later, 264 lost a Defiant in an accident when N3366 made a forced-landing one mile north-west of West Malling after engine failure during a test flight. The crew was safe and the Defiant was struck off charge after investigation. The consequences of the next accident, which occurred two days later on the 24th, were fatal for the crew. The pilot, Sgt W.G. Lewis, lost control during an air-to-ground gunnery practice and spun into the ground. It was the first fatality sustained by the squadron in eighteen months. During the first days of May, the squadron moved to Colerne to undertake conversion to the Mosquito Mk.II where a new CO took over with the rank of wing commander, Cooke reverting to a Flight commander position. The Defiants were progressively replaced by the twin-engine aircraft, while many changes of flying personnel took place. A handful of Defiants were retained until August (like AA400 and AA410), even though 264 was operational from mid-June on the Mosquito, marking the end of a two and a half year collaboration between the squadron and the turret fighter.

Defiant N1773 served with 264 Sqn between February and September 1941 as PS-H before being passed to 410 Sqn. This Defiant was often flown by P/O Gray and Sgt Hill during that time.
(*L.P. Russel via Paul Sortehaug*)

Date	Pilot	SN	Origin	Type	Serial	Code	Nb	Cat.
12.05.40	S/L Philip A. **Hunter**	RAF No. 32081	RAF	Ju88	**L6973**		0.33	C
	LAC Frederick H. **King**	RAF No. 523466	RAF					
	P/O Edward H. **Whitehouse**	RAF No. 42035	RAF		**L6972**		0.33	C
	Sgt Robert M. **Smalley**	RAF No. 581121	RAF					
	P/O Michael H. **Young**	RAF No. 42040	RAF		**L7003**		0.33	C
	LAC Stanley B. **Johnson**	RAF No. 747782	RAF					
	F/L Nicholas G. **Cooke**	RAF No.37652	RAF	He111	**L6975**		0.33*	C
	Cpl Albert **Lippett**	RAF No.348039	RAF					
	P/O Eric G. **Barwell**	RAF No.77454	RAF		**L6964**		0.33*	C
	Sgt **Quinney**	?	RAF					
13.05.40	P/O Patrick E.J. **Greenhous**	RAF No. 42000	RAF	Bf109	**L6977**	PS-U	1.0	C
	Sgt Frederick D. **Greenhalgh**	RAF No. 522982	RAF					
	P/O Samuel R. **Thomas**	RAF No.42029	RAF	Ju87	**L6958**		2.0	C
	LAC John S.M. **Bromley**	RAF No. 521432	RAF					
	P/O George F.A. **Skelton**	RAF No. 29147	(AUS)/RAF	Ju87	**L6969**	PS-B	1.0	C
	P/O John E. **Hatfield**	RAF No. 40474	(CAN)/RAF					
	P/O Alexander **MacLeod**	RAF No. 42013	RAF	Ju87	**L6965**		1.0	C
	LAC Walter E. **Cox**	RAF No. 747745	RAF					
24.05.40	P/O Edward H. **Whitehouse**	RAF No. 42035	RAF	Bf110	**L6972**		0.5	C
	P/O Horace **Scott**	RAF No. 77368	RAF					
	P/O David **Whitley**	RAF No. 42036	RAF		**L6961**		0.5	C
	LAC Robert C. **Turner**	RAF No.751362	RAF					
27.05.40	S/L Philip A. **Hunter**	RAF No. 32081	RAF	Bf109	**L6973**		1.0	C
	LAC Frederick H .**King**	RAF No. 523466	RAF					
	Sgt Edward R. **Thorn**	RAF No. 562610	RAF	Bf109	**L6986**		1.0	C
	LAC Frederick J. **Barker**	RAF No. 747751	RAF					
	P/O Michael H. **Young**	RAF No. 42040	RAF	Bf109	**L7003**		1.0	C
	LAC Stanley B. **Johnson**	RAF No. 747782	RAF					
	P/O Richard W. **Stokes**	RAF No. 42027	RAF	Bf109	**L6959**		0.5	C
	LAC Arthur L. **Fairbrother**	RAF No. 747317	RAF					
	P/O Michael H. **Young**	RAF No. 42040	RAF		**L7003**		0.5	C
	LAC Stanley B. **Johnson**	RAF No. 747782	RAF					
	P/O Edward H. **Whitehouse**	RAF No. 42035	RAF	He111	**L6972**		1.0	C
	P/O Horace **Scott**	RAF No. 77368	RAF					
	F/L Nicholas G. **Cooke**	RAF No. 37652	RAF	He111	**L7005**	PS-X	0.33	C
	Cpl Albert **Lippett**	RAF No. 348039	RAF					
	P/O Terence D. **Welsh**	RAF No. 42033	RAF		**L6964**		0.33	C
	LAC Laurence H. **Hayden**	RAF No. 749780	RAF					
	P/O David **Whitley**	RAF No. 42036	RAF		**L7004**		0.33	C
	LAC Robert C. **Turner**	RAF No. 751362	RAF					
	P/O Edward H. **Whitehouse**	RAF No. 42035	RAF	He111	**L6972**		0.5	C
	P/O Horace **Scott**	RAF No. 77368	RAF					
	P/O Michael H. **Young**	RAF No. 42040	RAF		**L7003**		0.5	C
	LAC Stanley B. **Johnson**	RAF No. 747782	RAF					
	S/L Philip A. **Hunter**	RAF No. 32081	RAF	He111	**L6973**		0.5	C
	LAC Frederick H .**King**	RAF No. 523466	RAF					
	P/O Michael H. **Young**	RAF No. 42040	RAF		**L7003**		0.5	C
	LAC Stanley B. **Johnson**	RAF No. 747782	RAF					
	F/L Nicholas G. **Cooke**	RAF No. 37652	RAF	He111	**L7005**	PS-X	0.33	C
	Cpl Albert **Lippett**	RAF No. 348039	RAF					

*Shared with No. 66 Sqn

Date	Name	RAF No.		Enemy	Serial	Code	Score	
	P/O David **Whitley**	RAF No. 42036	RAF		**L7004**		0.33	C
	LAC Robert C. **Turner**	RAF No. 751362	RAF					
	P/O Terence D. **Welsh**	RAF No. 42033	RAF		**L6964**		0.33	C
	LAC Laurence H. **Hayden**	RAF No. 749780	RAF					
28.05.40	S/L Philip A. **Hunter**	RAF No. 32081	RAF	Bf109	**L6973**		2.0	C
	LAC Frederick H. **King**	RAF No. 523466	RAF					
	Sgt Edward R. **Thorn**	RAF No. 562610	RAF	Bf109	**L6956**		3.0	C
	LAC Frederick J. **Barker**	RAF No. 747751	RAF					
	P/O Michael H. **Young**	RAF No. 42040	RAF	Bf109	**L7003**		1.0	C
	LAC Stanley B. **Johnson**	RAF No. 747782	RAF					
29.05.40	P/O Eric G. **Barwell**	RAF No. 77454	RAF	Bf109	**L7006**		1.0	C
	P/O John E.M. **Williams**	RAF No. 77370	RAF	Bf110			1.0	C
				Ju87			2.0	C
	P/O Terence D. **Welsh**	RAF No. 42033	RAF	Bf109	**L6964**		1.0	C
	LAC Laurence H. **Hayden**	RAF No. 749780	RAF	Bf110			1.0	C
				Ju87			2.0	C
	P/O Gerald H. **Hackwood**	RAF No. 42217	RAF	Bf109	**L6970**		1.0	C
	LAC George E. **Lille**	RAF No. 581462	RAF	Bf110			1.5	C
				Ju87			1.0	C
							0.5	C
							0.5	C
	P/O Michael H. **Young**	RAF No. 42040	RAF	Bf109	**L6967**	PS-P	1.0	C
	LAC Stanley B. **Johnson**	RAF No. 747782	RAF	Bf110			1.5	C
				Ju87			0.5	C
							0.5	C
				Ju88			0.33	C
	F/L Nicholas G. **Cooke**	RAF No. 37652	RAF	Bf109	**L7005**		3.0	C
	Cpl Albert **Lippett**	RAF No. 348039	RAF	Ju87			5.0	C
				Ju88			0.33	C
	S/L Philip A. **Hunter**	RAF No. 32081	RAF	Bf109	**L6973**		1.0	C
	LAC Frederick H. **King**	RAF No. 523466	RAF	Bf110			1.0	C
				Ju87			1.0	C
	Sgt Arnold J. **Lauder**	RAF No. 565601	RAF	Bf109	**L6972**		1.0	P
	LAC John F. **Wise**	RAF No. 746875						
	Sgt Edward R. **Thorn**	RAF No. 562610	RAF	Ju87	**L6956**		2.0	C
	LAC Frederick J. **Barker**	RAF No. 747751	RAF	Bf100			1.0	C
				Ju88			0.33	C
	P/O Desmond H.S. **Kay**	RAF No. 42006	RAF	Ju87	**L6961**		1.0	P
	LAC Walter E. **Cox**	RAF No. 747745	RAF					
	P/O Richard W. **Stokes**	RAF No. 42027	RAF	Ju87	**L6975**		1.0	C
	LAC Arthur L. **Fairbrother**	RAF No. 747317		Bf110			2.0	C
	P/O David **Whitley**	RAF No. 42036	RAF	Ju87	**L7004**		1.0	C
	LAC Robert C. **Turner**	RAF No. 751362	RAF					
31.05.40	P/O Eric G. **Barwell**	RAF No. 77454	RAF	Bf109	**L6972**		1.0	C
	P/O John E.M. **Williams**	RAF No. 77370	RAF	He111			1.0	C
	P/O Michael H. **Young**	RAF No. 42040	RAF	Bf109	**L6980**		1.0	C
	LAC Stanley B. **Johnson**	RAF No. 747782	RAF					
	S/L Philip A. **Hunter**	RAF No. 32081	RAF	Bf109	**L6973**		1.0	C
	LAC Frederick H. **King**	RAF No. 523466	RAF	He111			1.0	C
	P/O Guy L. **Hickman**	RAF No. 4225	RAF	Bf109	**L6968**		1.0	P
	LAC Alfred **Fidler**	RAF No. 743039	RAF					
	P/O Gerald H. **Hackwood**	RAF No. 42217	RAF	He111	**L6970**		2.5	C
	LAC George E. **Lille**	RAF No. 581462	RAF					
	Sgt Edward R. **Thorn**	RAF No. 562610	RAF	He111	**L6966**		1.5	C
	LAC Frederick J. **Barker**	RAF No. 747751	RAF					
15.08.40	P/O David **Whitley**	RAF No. 42036	RAF	He111	**L6985**		1.0	C
	Sgt Robert C. **Turner**	RAF No. 751362	RAF					
24.08.40	S/L George D. **Garvin**	RAF No. 34237	RAF	Ju88	**L7025**	PS-Z	1.0	C

Date	Name	Service No.	Force	Aircraft	Serial	Code	Score	
	F/L Robert C.V. **ASH**	RAF No. 31023	RAF					
	P/O David **WHITLEY**	RAF No. 42036	RAF	Ju88	**L7021**	PS-H	1.0	C
	Sgt Robert C. **TURNER**	RAF No. 751362	RAF					
	Sgt Edward R. **THORN**	RAF No. 562610	RAF	Ju88	**L7003**		1.0	C
	Sgt Frederick J. **BARKER**	RAF No. 747751	RAF					
	P/O Eric G. **BARWELL**	RAF No. 77454	RAF	Bf109	**L7026**	PS-V	1.0	C
	Sgt A. **MARTIN**	?	RAF					
	S/L George D. **GARVIN**	RAF No. 34237	RAF	Ju88	**L7025**	PS-Z	2.0	C
	F/L Robert C.V. **ASH**	RAF No. 31023	RAF					
	P/O Terence D. **WELSH**	RAF No. 42033	RAF	Ju88	**L7003**		1.0	C
	Sgt Laurence H. **HAYDEN**	RAF No. 749780	RAF					
	P/O Terence D. **WELSH**	RAF No. 42033	RAF	Ju88	**L7003**		1.0	C
	Sgt Laurence H. **HAYDEN**	RAF No. 749780	RAF					
	P/O Michael H. **YOUNG**	RAF No. 42040	RAF	He111	**L7005**	PS-X	1.0	C
	Sgt Leslie P. **RUSSELL**	NZ40209	RNZAF					
26.08.40	Sgt Edward R. **THORN**	RAF No. 562610	RAF	Bf109	**L7005**	PS-X	1.0	C
	Sgt Frederick J. **BARKER**	RAF No. 747751	RAF					
	P/O Frederick D. **HUGUES**	RAF No. 74706	RAF	Do17	**L7028**		2.0	C
	Sgt Fred **GASH**	RAF No. 967911	RAF					
	P/O Howard I. **GOODALL**	RAF No.79159	RAF	Do17	**L7024**		1.0	C
	Sgt Robert B.M. **YOUNG**	NZ40197	RNZAF					
	Sgt Edward R. **THORN**	RAF No. 562610	RAF	Do17	**L7005**	PS-X	2.0	C
	Sgt Frederick J. **BARKER**	RAF No. 747751	RAF					
	F/L Arthur J. **BANHAM**	RAF No. 37565	RAF	Do17	**L6985**		1.0	C
	Sgt Barrie **BAKER**	RAF No. 935961	RAF					
28.08.40	P/O William F. **CARNABY**	AAF No. 90157	RAF	He111	**N1576**		1.0	C
	P/O Cyril C. **ELLERY**	RAF No. 78747	RAF					
12.03.41	P/O Frederick D. **HUGUES**	RAF No. 74706	RAF	He111	**N1801**	PS-Y	1.0	C
	Sgt Fred **GASH**	RAF No. 967911	RAF					
	P/O Terence D. **WELSH**	RAF No. 42033	RAF	He111	**N1672**		1.0	C
	Sgt Laurence H. **HAYDEN**	RAF No. 749780	RAF					
08.04.41	S/L Arthur T.D. **SANDERS**	RAF No. 33095	RAF	He111	**N3377**		1.0	C
	P/O Frederick C. **SUTTON**	RAF No. 79197	RAF					
09.04.41	P/O Terence D. **WELSH**	RAF No. 42033	RAF	He111	**N1801**	PS-Y	1.0	P
	Sgt Laurence H. **HAYDEN**	RAF No. 749780	RAF					
10.04.41	P/O Eric G. **BARWELL**	RAF No. 77454	RAF	Ju88	**N3367**		1.0	C
	Sgt A. **MARTIN**	?	RAF					
11.04.41	P/O Eric G. **BARWELL**	RAF No. 77454	RAF	He111	**N3367**		1.0	P
	Sgt A. **MARTIN**	?	RAF					
	P/O Frederick D. **HUGUES**	RAF No. 74706	RAF	He111	**N3353**		1.0	C
	Sgt Fred **GASH**	RAF No. 967911	RAF					
07.05.41	P/O Edward G. **CURTICE**	RAF No. 79203	RAF	He111	**N3326**		1.0	C
	P/O Peter C. **CAMPBELL-MARTIN**	RAF No. 78357	RAF					
	P/O Gerald J. **GRAY**	RAF No. 88209	RAF	He111	**N3368**		1.0	C
	P/O Stephen E. **HILL**	RAF No. 85705	RAF					
08.05.41	P/O Michael H. **YOUNG**	RAF No. 42040	RAF	Bf110	**N3377**	PS-J	1.0	C
	Sgt Leslie P. **RUSSELL**	NZ40209	RNZAF					
10.05.41	S/L Arthur T.D. **SANDERS**	RAF No. 33095	RAF	He111	**N3313**	PS-P	1.0	C
	P/O Frederick C. **SUTTON**	RAF No. 79197	RAF					
	F/L Ian R. **STEPHENSON**	RAF No. 72010	RAF	He111	**N3370**		1.0	C
	P/O Mervyn H. **MAGGS**	RAF No. 79357	RAF					
	P/O Edward G. **CURTICE**	RAF No. 79203	RAF	Do17	**N3326**		1.0	C
	P/O Peter C. **CAMPBELL-MARTIN**	RAF No. 78357	RAF					
17.04.42	P/O Anthony I. **STUART**	Aus. 403383	RAAF	He111	**AA420***		1.0	C
	P/O Mervyn H. **MAGGS**	RAF No. 79357	RAF					

Mk II

Total: 102.33

The most successful Defiant crew was that of Ted Thorn (left) and Fred Barker (right). The latter was also the RAF's most successful air gunner of the war. (*via Andrew Thomas*)

Summary of the aircraft lost on Operations - 264 Squadron

Date	Pilot	S/N	Origin	Serial	Code	Fate
13.05.40	F/L George F.A. **Skelton**	RAF No. 29147	(AUS)/RAF	**L6969**	PS-B	**PoW**
	P/O Jack E. **Hatfield**	RAF No. 40474	(CAN)/RAF			-
	P/O Gordon E. **Chandler**	RAF No. 33559	RAF	**L6960**	PS-M	†
	LAC Douglas L. **McLeish**	RAF No. 581467	RAF			†
	P/O Samuel R. **Thomas**	RAF No. 42029	RAF	**L6958**		**Eva.**
	LAC John S.M. **Bromley**	RAF No. 521432	RAF			†
	P/O Patrick E.J. **Greenhous**	RAF No. 42000	RAF	**L6977**	PS-U	**PoW**
	Sgt Frederick D. **Greenhalgh**	RAF No.522982	RAF			**PoW**
	P/O Alexander **McLeod**	RAF No. 42013	RAF	**L6965**		**Eva.**
	LAC Walter E. **Cox**	RAF No. 747745	RAF			**Eva.**
28.05.40	F/L Edward H. **Whitehouse**	RAF No. 42035	RAF	**L6959**		†
	P/O Horace **Scott**	RAF No.77368	RAF			†
	P/O Alexander **McLeod**	RAF No. 42013	RAF	**L7007**		†
	P/O Jack E. **Hatfield**	RAF No. 40474	(CAN)/RAF			†
	Sgt Lionel C.W. **Daisley**	RAF No. 741278	RAF	**L6953**		†
	LAC Harold **Revill**	RAF No. 747795	RAF			†
31.05.40	P/O David **Whitley**	RAF No. 42036	RAF	**L6961**		-
	LAC Robert C. **Turner**	RAF No. 751362	RAF			-
	P/O Michael H. **Young**	RAF No. 42040	RAF	**L6980**		-
	LAC Stanley B. **Johnson**	RAF No. 747782	RAF			†
	P/O Guy L. **Hickman**	RAF No. 42225	RAF	**L6968**		†
	LAC Alfred **Fidler**	RAF No. 743039	RAF			†
	F/L Nicholas G. **Cooke**	RAF No. 37652	RAF	**L6975**		†
	Cpl Albert **Lippett**	RAF No. 348039	RAF			†
	P/O Eric G. **Barwell**	RAF No. 77454	RAF	**L6972**		-
	P/O John E.M. **Williams**	RAF No. 77370	RAF			-

Date	Name	No.	Service	Serial	Code	Fate
24.08.40	P/O David **Whitley**	RAF No. 42036	RAF	**L6996**	PS-L	-
	Sgt Robert C. **Turner**	RAF No. 751362	RAF			-
	P/O Joseph T. **Jones**	RAF No. 78855	RAF	**L6966**		†
	P/O William A. **Ponting**	RAF No. 79217	RAF			†
	F/O Ian G. **Shaw**	RAF No. 40265	RAF	**L7027**		†
	Sgt Alan **Berry**	RAF No. 968035	RAF			†
	S/L Philip A. **Hunter**	RAF No. 32081	RAF	**N1535**	PS-A	†
	P/O Frederick H. **King**	RAF No. 43845	RAF			†
	P/O Richard S. **Gaskell**	RAF No. 42832	RAF	**L6965**		-
	Sgt William H. **Machin**	RAF No. 968717	RAF			†
26.08.40	F/L Arthur J. **Banham**	RAF No.37565	RAF	**L6985**		-
	Sgt Barrie **Baker**	RAF No. 935961	RAF			-
	Sgt Edward R. **Thorn**	RAF No. 562610	RAF	**L7005**	PS-X	-
	Sgt Frederick J. **Barker**	RAF No. 747751	RAF			-
	F/O Ian R. **Stephenson**	RAF No. 72010	RAF	**L7025**	PS-Z	-
	Sgt Walter **Maxwell**	RAF No. 967872	RAF			†
28.08.40	S/L George D. **Gavin**	RAF No. 34237	RAF	**L7026**	PS-L	-
	F/L Robert C.V. **Ash**	RAF No. 31023	RAF			†
	P/O David **Whitley**	RAF No. 42036	RAF	**N1574**		†
	Sgt Robert C. **Turner**	RAF No. 751362	RAF			†
	P/O Peter L. **Kenner**	RAF No. 73032	RAF	**L7021**	PS-H	†
	P/O Charles E. **Johnson**	RAF No. 79241	RAF			†
04.09.40	P/O Derek K.C. **O'Malley**	RAF No. 72475	RAF	**N1628**		†
	Sgt Lauritz A.W. **Rasmussen**	NZ391868	RNZAF			†
08.10.40	P/O Harold I. **Goodall**	RAF No. 79159	RAF	**N1627**		†
	Sgt Robert B.M. **Young**	NZ40197	RNZAF			†
15.11.40	P/O William R.A. **Knocker**	RAF No. 74333	RAF	**N1547**		-
	P/O Frank A. **Toombs**	RAF No. 79221	RAF			†
20.11.40	P/O Gerald H. **Hackwood**	RAF No. 42217	RAF	**N1626**		†
	F/O Alexander J. **Storrie**	RAF No. 43641	RAF			†
08.03.41	F/O James C. **Melvill**	RAF No. 74681	RAF	**N3478**		-
	Sgt Wilfred L. **Butler**	RAF No. 645433	RAF			-
15.04.41	P/O William R.A. **Knocker**	RAF No. 74333	RAF	**N3369**		-
	Sgt Oswald A. **Hardy**	RAF No. 968245	RAF			-

Total: 30

Despite some early successes, fighting against the Luftwaffe was a dangerous game for the Defiant. L6957/PS-T was bounced by Bf109s on 29 May 1940 and P/O D.H.S. Kay was lucky to get back to base. However, the gunner, LAC E.J. Jones, a Canadian, had bailed out and was posted missing. His body was later found on a French beach. Note the damage that was probably caused by a shell from a 20mm cannon, a deadly and efficient weapon in 1940.

Left: portrait of P/O Gordon E. Chandler, one of the first Defiant pilots to be killed in action on 13 May, and, right, P/O Patrick Greenhous who became a PoW the same day. *(via Ja Jolie)*

Summary of the aircraft lost by accident - 264 Squadron

Date	Pilot	S/N	Origin	Serial	Code	Fate
23.04.40	P/O Patrick E.G. **Greenhous**	RAF No. 42000	RAF	**L6952**		-
	LAC John S.M. **Bromley**	RAF No. 521432	RAF			-
07.06.40	P/O William F. **Carnaby**	AAF No. 90157	RAF	**L7004**		-
	P/O Cyril C. **Ellery**	RAF No. 78747	RAF			-
11.06.40	P/O George A. **Hutcheson**	RAF No. 79161	RAF	**L6970**		†
	LAC Gerald **Robinson**	RAF No. 591179	RAF			-
07.10.40	P/O Gerald H. **Hackwood**	RAF No. 42217	RAF	**N1578**		-
	P/O Anthony **O'Connell**	RAF No. 42260	RAF			-
22.04.41	Sgt Anthony D. **Lofting**	RAF No. 1313191	RAF	**N3366**		-
	-					
31.08.41	P/O William R.A. **Knocker**	RAF No. 74333	RAF	**N3453**		-
	F/Sgt Oswald A. **Hardy**	RAF No. 968245	RAF			-
07.09.41	Sgt Ludwik **Tokarczyk+**	PAF No. 793641	PAF	**N4049**		-
	-					
26.04.42	Sgt Wallace G. **Lewis**	AUS. 404565	RAAF	**AA377***		†
	F/Sgt William **Mair**	RAF No. 971422	RAF			†

+Not a 264 Sqn pilot, sent by ATA to ferry the Defiant. The accident is not reported in the Squadron's ORB, so the Defiant might be already considered as not being part of 264's inventory anymore.

** Mk II*

Total: 8

Peter Townsend would continue to lead 85 Sqn while it was equipped with the Havoc and would be awarded the DSO in May 1941. He later commanded 605 Sqn, a night intruder unit, and in February 1944 was appointed Equerry to King George VI.

No. 85 Squadron (code VY)

A Hurricane squadron since 1938, 85 fought brilliantly in France and during the Battle of Britain as a day fighter squadron before it switched to the night fighting role the following autumn. It was commanded by Squadron Leader Peter Townsend who had led the unit since May. In January 1941, the squadron was stationed at Debden, north of London, and took charge of Defiants to complement its Hurricanes. Nine were received in the first days of January (N1803, N1805, N3327, N3338, N3374, N3389, N3433, N3434 and N3436). The CO made the squadron's first Defiant flight on the 4th and gave favourable reports on the type's handling. However, the switch from the Hurricane to the Defiant was not met with great enthusiasm by the pilots who saw their new role as taxi-drivers for the air gunners. With the arrival of the gunners, the squadron had to work out how a crew would work together. Training was carried out during the month as far as weather permitted, snow fell many times during the month, and things went smoothly with nothing special to report except that Townsend received a Bar to his DFC and, on the 21st, the squadron was warned that it would be re-equipped with Havoc night fighters. In January, only 140 hours of training flights were achieved, mainly on Defiants. On 4 February, orders were received to hand over the Defiants to No. 96 Squadron. The big change occurred on the 15th when the pilots of 96 Squadron arrived to collect the Defiants while the first Havoc arrived the same day. A few days earlier, 85 had the opportunity to send their Defiants on three uneventful operational patrols in conjunction with its Hurricanes. These would be the only operational flights carried out by 85 Squadron's Defiants.

No. 96 Squadron (code ZJ):

Number 96 Squadron was formed on 18 December 1940 from No. 422 Flight. This Flight had been formed two months previously to study the use of single-seat night fighters and was equipped with Hurricanes. Based at Shoreham, near Brighton, the Flight moved on 9 December to Cranage, south of Manchester, in preparation for its formation into a squadron. The experiment had been successful as the Flight claimed two enemy aircraft destroyed and one damaged in six weeks. Command of the new squadron was given to Squadron Leader R.G. Kellett, a Battle of Britain veteran. The unit's aircraft remained the Hurricane at first, but it was planned that 96 would become a Defiant unit, as the type was now relegated to night fighter duties. The transition to the Defiant was slow, the first aircraft to arrive was N3389 on 15 January 1941, followed in February by N1766, N1767, N1803, N3327, N3338, N3374, N3433, N3434, N3436, with air gunners posted in at the same time. The full complement of Defiants was finally received

in March and April. The squadron flew both the Defiant and Hurricane until May and, at that time, S/L Kellett relinquished command to S/L R.J. Burns, a South African. The first operational flight of a Defiant was completed on the night of 12/13 March, the CO flying N3338, and Sgt Ralls in N3376, to patrol over Liverpool. Other Defiants took off that night, as did some Hurricanes, with one of the latter destroying a He111. The Defiant crews were not that lucky as Defiant N1803, flown by Czech F/O Vesely and gunner Sgt Haycock, was hit by return fire wounding the pilot. Defiant T3954, flown by a New Zealand crew (Sgts Taylor and Broughton), was also unlucky as the guns jammed after only six rounds and the He111 they had intercepted was not damaged. They decided to fol-

Victor Verity was among the highly skilled pilots to join 96 Sqn when the unit formed. A New Zealander, he applied for a short service commission in the RAF in 1938. When war broke out, he was still under training, but by the end of 1939 he had joined 229 Sqn. In May 1940, he was attached to 615 Sqn and participated in the Battle of France, but was soon shot down and evacuated to England. Rejoining his squadron, he fought in the Battle of Britain and in October he joined 422 Flt which became 96 Sqn soon after. He left 96 in August 1941 for a rest. He later completed a second tour in the Middle East with 89 and 108 Sqns, flying night fighter sorties, and ended the war with a DFC, nine confirmed victories, three probables and five damaged. He left the RAF in November 1945.

(VBS Verity via Paul Sortehaug)

Defiant T3954/ZJ-K arrived at the squadron in March 1941, but its tenure was short and it left one month later. During that short period of time, it was mainly flown by the CO, South African Robert Burns, and his gunner, P/O Smith. A pre-war RAF pilot, Burns had served in various HQ positions between the declaration of war and assuming command of the squadron (his only operational position). Continuing his career with the RAF after the war, he eventually reached the rank of air commodore. *(Andrew Thomas)*

low the German bomber to at least try to disrupt its activities. The hunt continued until the Heinkel flew into a bank of cloud at 1,000 feet, too dangerous a height with the Welsh mountains around. The rest of the month was rather uneventful despite continuous sorties (34 recorded on Defiants).

The month of April started as March ended with bad weather limiting training and operational activity alike until the 7th. During the month, the Hurricanes were progressively discarded, and, surprisingly, the Defiant had become the favourite aircraft for most of the pilots. During the night of the 11th, two Defiants took off to practice interceptions, one playing a bomber, the other the fighter. All went well until the aircraft playing the fighter was suddenly attacked by an unknown aircraft. The Kiwi crew of Sgts Taylor and Broughton took evasive action and opened fire in reply. The right wing and the fuselage were holed but the Defiant managed to return to base. The New Zealander crew had had a close encounter with a Beaufighter! A combat report was filed to prevent an incident like this happening again, but the case didn't go beyond that. Two days later, the squadron lost its first Defiant when, during a test flight, the engine of N1766 failed and the crew were forced to abandon the aircraft. Both landed safely by parachute. On the positive side, there was little to record during the month. There was a visual contact by the Sgt Angell/Sgt Goldsmith crew on 15/16 April, but the Luftwaffe was not very active in the area at the time. Sadly, that crew would be killed less than two weeks later when they were near Digby while flying a night cross-country exercise. The black days didn't stop, however, and a third Defiant was lost in April. N3376 lost its engine during a night flight test. The crew bailed out successfully.

Early in May, the Hurricanes made their last operational sorties (some would be kept for training). After a disastrous April, May was much better for morale. On 6/7 May, the F/O V.S.S. Verity/Sgt F.W. Wake took off for a patrol at 0025. The first half-hour was uneventful except puffs of AA fire. Then Verity saw a Defiant and almost immediately afterwards a twin-engined aircraft which he lost while trying to manoeuvre into positon. While at 13,000 feet, he spotted a He111 about 4,000 feet below him. Diving down slightly to the right of the enemy aircraft, he gave his gunner the opportunity to open fire with one second burst at 50 yards range into the right engine from below. Having slightly overshot, he banked to the left and gave his gunner another chance to fire a burst into the front of the cockpit this time. During this burst, there was a violent explosion enveloping the whole of the Heinkel and when Verity and Wake had recovered their sight, the Heinkel had disappeared. He was claimed as destroyed. A few minutes later, a second engagement took place with a Ju88 but it was unconclusive and the German bomber was claimed as damaged while in the same time, Sergeant A.E. Scott in a Hurricane claimed one He111 as a probable. Other visual contacts were made that night but no further combats followed. The next night, Sergeant Scott, teamed this time with Sgt Streeter, later claimed one He111 destroyed. The squadron was very successful that night with two other crews making claims. Flying Officer Verity and his gunner claimed one Ju88 destroyed and another probably destroyed after firing 1034 rounds. One He111 destroyed and another damaged of Dornier type were claimed by Sgt Taylor (RNZAF) and his gunner, Sgt McCormack. The latter fired 700 rounds during the two combats. Also, Sgt McNair and his gunner had two combats that night, but made no claim. Despite more than 100 sorties flown in May, no further claims were made. No incidents or accidents were reported either. After an intensive month, June was very quiet with the forty sorties only being a third of the previous month's total. Besides a Ju88 damaged by S/L Burns and his gunner, F/O W. Smith, around

Wirral on 1/2 June, and a He111 damaged on 24/25 June by Sgt R. Smithson and his gunner, nothing happened in June. The Luftwaffe was not flying in the area and had actually left for the future Eastern front, so activity was at a minimum. That also led to a kind of frustration as the diarist wrote "Cranage would be a good place for those who don't want to fly"! In July, only 34 sorties were recorded and only fifteen in August! Despite this, the squadron lost a number of aircraft and crew. On 22 July, Defiant T4071 crashed during an air test and both crewmen were killed, including Richard Smithson who was recently commissioned. He was a Battle of Britain veteran, having fought with 249 Sqn, and had joined 96 on its formation in December 1940. In August, three more Defiants were lost on non-operational flights: T3924 on 2 August (the pilot, P/O J. Keprt, was injured, but his air gunner was not); N3447, both crew killed; and finally N3383 was lost after an engine failure with both crew injured in the crash. In September, the squadron did not fly any Defiants on ops because of rather bad weather for a large part of the month and a lack of enemy activity. Training and co-operation flights became the routine for the month on either Defiants or the last remaining Hurricanes. October was a bit better and sixteen Defiant sorties were logged. The rest of the time was spent in training and co-operation duties. However, contrary to the previous month, which was free of any major incidents or accidents, two Defiants were wrecked. The first loss occurred on 16 October during a training exercise. Pilot Officer M.G. Hilton and his air gunner, Sgt W. Brunkhorst (RAAF), hit a hill top about 400 yards from the Cat & Fiddle Inn near Buxton. They survived the crash. Injured, they were found twelve hours later the following morning meandering down a road heading to Buxton. It was to be the last major event before the unit moved to Wexhram south of Liverpool on the 21ˢᵗ. It would be from there that all of the operational activity for the month mentioned earlier would take place (about ten unsuccessful interception attempts) as well as the second loss of the month. At 20.55 on 25 October, Pilot Officer J.J. Phoenix and his air gunner Sgt Seales took off for an operational patrol, but during the take off run the Defiant (T3999) struck a gooseneck flare, seriously damaged the elevator and the ailerons. With great care, Phoenix continued the take off, climbed to 6,000 feet and both men took to their parachutes. In November, the squadron was close to resembling a paratrooper training school with two more crews bailing out from their Defiants! On 3 November, while on a CGI exercise over North Wales in the middle of the night (they had taken off at 01.40), Defiant T4008, flown by the CO, suffered a wireless failure resulting in the crew becoming lost before they bailed out at 6,500 feet. They were found later in the morning. The air gunner was unlucky as he broke an ankle on landing. Soon after, two Defiants were sent to locate the missing aircraft, but the engine of N1575 caught fire in flight and the crew was also forced to abandon their aircraft. It was only a bit better for the second Defiant whose crew became lost in bad weather and chose to make a forced landing. They escaped injury and the Defiant sustained only slight damage and was repaired. Otherwise, November was relatively uneventful with no operational sorties carried out. With winter approaching, no one could expect much operational flying and during the following months the activity remained limited. In mid-December, the CO was promoted to wing commander and left the squadron to take command of the MFSU. He was replaced by S/L R.C. Haines who was posted from No. 68 Squadron where he had been a flight commander. He had also served with No. 600 Squadron during the Battle of

Defiant T4052/ZJ-H at its dispersal at Cranage during a spring evening in 1941. Other aircraft known to be on strength at that time were N3374/A, N3376/E and T3923/J.

Britain and was a DFC recipient. Before leaving, Burns would make the last sortie (and the only one for December) on the evening of the 11th when he unsuccessfully tried to intercept an enemy aircraft coming into the Sector area. Winter was spent in training and no operational flights were achieved in January, February and March 1942. One radar-equipped Defiant Mk.I stalled on approach after a test flight on 17 February. Both crew were killed in the crash. Since the end of 1941, the squadron had begun to receive Defiants fitted with AI which improved their chances for successful interceptions. From mid-March 1942, Defiant Mk.IIs fitted with AI started to arrive with the first four being AA542, AA574, AA575 and AA577. By the end of April, the squadron was equipped with sixteen Defiant Mk.IIs. One of those, AA546, would have a short stay as it was issued to the squadron on 27 April and lost in a crash, while on a co-operation flight simulating low flying attack, on 27 May. The pilot was killed, but Pilot Officer B.S. Cadman, who was seated in the turret, was uninjured. In April, with the weather improving, more flights were flown, but only three operational patrols, two on 25 April and another three days later. These would be the last operational sorties logged on Defiants for a total of close to 300 since the formation of the squadron. That same month, the crews learned the squadron, like many other Defiant units, would be converted to Beaufighters. The first Beau arrived in May along with Blenheims for twin-engine conversions. On 30 May, the squadron became officially non-operational and the Defiants progressively departed. At the same time, the crews were happy to see the return of W/C Burns, a Beaufighter unit required a wing commander, while S/L Haines took over as head of A Flight. A new chapter for the squadron was about to begin. The 96 would have flown less 300 sorties in Defiant.

Claims - 96 Squadron (Confirmed and Probable)

Date	Pilot	SN	Origin	Type	Serial	Code	Nb	Cat.
07.05.41	F/O Victor B.S. **VERITY**	RAF No. 42164	(NZ)/RAF	He111	**N1803**		1.0	C
	Sgt Frederick W. **WAKE**	RAF No. 905920	RAF					
08.05.41	Sgt Alfred E. **SCOTT**	RAF No. 815013	RAF	He111	**N3327**		1.0	C
	Sgt William E. **STREETER**	RAF No. 934638	RAF					
	F/O Victor B.S. **VERITY**	RAF No. 42164	(NZ)/RAF	Ju88	**N1803**		1.0	C
	Sgt Frederick W. **WAKE**	RAF No. 905920	RAF					
	Sgt George S. **TAYLOR**	NZ391849	RNZAF	He111	**T3923**	ZJ-J	1.0	C
	Sgt John B. **MCCORMACK**	RAF No. 625013	RAF					

Total: 4.00

Summary of the aircraft lost on Operations - 96 Squadron

Date	Pilot	S/N	Origin	Serial	Code	Fate
22.10.41	P/O Joseph I. **PHOENIX**	RAF No. 66591	RAF	**T3999**		-
	Sgt Leslie **SEALES**	RAF No. 906317	RAF			-

Total: 1

Summary of the aircraft lost by accident - 96 Squadron

Date	Pilot	S/N	Origin	Serial	Code	Fate
13.04.41	F/L Paul W. **RABONE**	RAF No. 36179	(NZ)/RAF	**N1766**		-
	F/O John M. **RITCHIE**	RAF No. 79193	RAF			-
27.04.41	Sgt Walter B. **ANGELL**	RAF No. 916859	RAF	**N3389**		†
	Sgt John E. **GOLDSMITH**	RAF No. 901859	RAF			†
30.04.41	Sgt Leslie F. **RALLS**	RAF No. 590723	RAF	**N3376**	ZJ-E	-
	Sgt **PHILP**	?	?			-
02.08.41	P/O Josef **KEPRT**	RAF No. 68138	(CZ)/RAF	**T3924**	ZJ-H	-
	Sgt Thomas A.W. **HARPER**	No. 9690373	RAF			-
22.07.41	P/O Richard **SMITHSON**	RAF No. 46174	RAF	**T4071**	ZJ-P	†
	Sgt Ivan N. **ROBINSON**	NZ40208	RNZAF			†
05.08.41	P/O John R. **DUNCAN**	RAF No. 91964	RAF	**N3447**		†
	F/Sgt Frederick A. **ALLCROFT**	RAF No. 902259	RAF			†
31.08.41	P/O Ernest H. **JACOB**	RAF No. 61961	RAF	**N3383**		-
	Sgt Arnold F. **ARNOLD**	CAN./ R.65508	RCAF			-
16.10.41	P/O Michael G. **HILTON**	RAF No. 66587	RAF	**T3921**		-
	Sgt Howard W. **BRUNKHORST**	AUS. 404438	RAAF			-
03.11.41	S/L Robert J.B. **BURNS**	RAF No. 34142	(SA)/RAF	**T4008**		-
	F/O Walter R. **SMITH**	RAF No. 44685	RAF			-
	F/O Victor B.S. **VERITY**	RAF No. 42164	(NZ)/RAF	**N1575**		-
	Sgt R. **ARMSTONG**	?	?			-
17.02.42	P/O Denis P. **SMITH**	RAF No. 106189	RAF	**AA319**		†
	LAC Malcolm G. **STEED**	RAF No. 1400753	RAF			†
27.05.42	P/O Robert B. **BOWRAN**	RAF No. 106138	RAF	**AA546***		†
	P/O Bernard S. **CADMAN**	RAF No. 119115	RAF			-

** Mk II*

Total: 12

When a new operational squadron was formed, some experienced personnel were posted in. For 125 Sqn, this rule was applied and among the pilots who joined was F/L Eric Barwell who had served with 264 Sqn over Dunkirk in May 1940. While he didn't add any claims to his score while flying the Defiant, he would do so once the unit converted to the Beaufighter and Mosquito. He ended the war as WingCo Flying of 148 Wing, with a Bar to his DFC and nine confirmed victories, one probable and one damaged (plus one V-1 destroyed). He was released from the RAF in September 1945.

A Defiant of 125 Sqn being re-armed - in vain as no claims were made by the squadron during its Defiant era.

No. 125 (Newfoundland) Squadron (code VA):

The formation of 125 Squadon was quick. Officially formed at Colerne on 16 June 1941, the first CO, S/L H.M. Mitchell, a former Battle of Britain veteran who had been awarded the DFC the previous October and had fought recently with No. 25 Squadron, a night fighter unit, arrived two days later. By the end of the month, twelve Defiants were taken on charge (N1748, N3384, N3428, N3485, N3489, N3493, N3499, T3951, T3986, T4074 and T4076), but the arrival of the crews took a bit more time. Early in July came the flight commanders: Flight Lieutenant T.D. Welsh DFC, from No. 264 Squadron and a very experienced Defiant pilot who had been flying on the type since spring 1940; and Flight Lieutenant E.G. Barwell, another DFC recipient and Welsh's squadron-mate. With the full complement of aircrew and aircraft, training was carried out during the summer. The first fatal accident was recorded on 16 August when N3499 dived into the ground when control was lost in low cloud after take off from Colerne. The pilot, Sgt H.L. Learning from Newfoundland, was killed. It seems that he was flying alone as no air gunner was reported as safe, injured or killed. Three days later, Sgt R. Bastow and Sgt A.G. Davis were forced to abandon their Defiant (T4110) after becoming lost while on a searchlight co-operation exercise. Training continued in September and eventually the squadron became operational on the 27th. The first three patrols were flown two evenings later, the CO taking off first at 22.50 and returning at 01.00. An unidentified aircraft was reported, but it soon became apparent that it was a friendly aircraft. Otherwise, nothing was reported that night, nor the next one when two more patrols were flown, the last for September. On September 30, while returning from a training flight, a tyre burst on landing at Fairwood Common, Defiant N1681 hit boulders and the undercarriage collapsed. The crew, Sgts A.G. Olley, pilot, and P. Temple, air gunner, was unhurt and the aircraft was sent for repairs. After an assessment, the aircraft was converted to instructional airframe 2981M and eventually SOC the following June. Early in October, now stationed at Fairwood Common, north of Swansea, the squadron received its first Defiant Mk.II, AA437. There was no plan to receive further Mk.IIs so AA437 was transferred to 264 Squadron. That month, twenty operational patrols were carried out, but the squadron struck three Defiants - T4104 on the 21st, T4040 on the 22nd and T3985 on the 25th – from its inventory and for the latter New Zealander Sgt C.A.G. Dale was killed. The Defiant had taken off for an operational patrol when his Defiant hit a balloon cable three minutes after being airborne. If both crew bailed out, only the air gunner survived. Among the casualties reported, there was also Sergeant E.J. Harrington who was badly burned in the crash of the 22nd (T4040) that resulted from a ground collision with a Hurricane from No. 79 Squadron. In October, three other accidents were also recorded, but the aircraft were repairable.

In November the number of patrols increased to 45, but no engagement was recorded despite many enemy aircraft being spotted. Similarly, there were no mishaps. A new flight commander arrived on the 11th, F/L A.N. Constantine, an Australian serving in the RAF, formerly of 264 Squadron, who arrived to take over A Flight. On 1 December, F/L Barwell took over the squadron, retaining command of B Flight at the same time. After Christmas, other changes occurred. Flight Lieutenant Constantine left for 87 Squadron and two new flight commanders were posted in, F/L D.P. Wade, from 247 Squadron and F/L J.R.L. Bailey from 264. During that month, the squadron, despite repeated patrols, escorts of shipping and dusk sweeps, fifty sorties in all, was again unfortunate to not bring any German aircraft down. It was frustrating for the personnel. It was partly due to bad weather, but also because the Germans had chosen an indirect approach to the area, avoiding the sector controlled by 125. When vectored on to a bandit, the Defiants arrived too late to achieve a successful interception.

In January, winds of change blew when a Blenheim Mk.I and an Airspeed Oxford arrived on the 24th followed by Wing Commander D.V. Ivins on the 29th (posted from 1451 Flight). That was the prelude to the conversion to the Beaufighter. It meant that S/L Barwell had to relinquish command to W/C Ivins, returning to a flight commander position with a multi-engine squadron. On the operational side, the squadron flew 112 times and, as with the previous month, no interceptions were made despite intense enemy activity. On 24 January, the squadron returned to Colerne. A Flight remained at Fairwood Common for another fortnight while the first Beaufighter Mk.IIs were taken on charge. Operational flying on Defiants ceased on 8 February, after 248 frustratingly unsuccessful sorties on Defiant, to allow the personnel to focus on the conversion to the Beau. The Defiants would remain in the squadron's inventory until it became operational on Beaufighters in April. But the Defiant would leave the squadon in the high way. On the night 25/26 April, two consecutive night raids were made to Bath, the first before midnight and the second about 05.00 hours the followling morning. The Beaufighter became operational the first night. The following night another raid took place which ended before 03.00 hours and some extra crews borrowed Defiant and Hurricane aircraft to patrol directly over the target area. Wing Commander Ivins in an Hurricane had two or three visuals on enemy aircraft and attacked from astern at 200 yards. Strikes were observed on the German bomber which appeared to be a Do217 and was claimed as damaged. The Newfoundlander Pilot Officer 'Ran' White and his gunner, the New Zealander Pilot Officer J.R. Gavegan, were more fortunate. They identified a Heinkel 111 against a background of light cloud 2,000 feet above crossing the tail of the Defiant at right angles, from left to right. White climbed to the left side of the enemy aircraft keeping it between the moon and himself. He attacked it at a range of 50 feet, pieces being observed to fly off the Heinkel. A further attack was later made with now large pieces were seen to blow off and the fuselage set aglow from wing-root to tail. The Heinkel was claimed as probably destroyed. Sergeant P. Gruchy from Newfoundland and Pilot Officer L. Langley, his gunner, attacked a Heinkel 111 in a Defiant (N1730) too and held there fire until a point blank range but unfortunately the guns did not fire owing to the 'firing safe' mechanism was missing. That was due to hurried servicing of many unserviceable aircraft to counter the raid. Three other Defiants were also airborne that night but no encounters were made.

Claims - 125 Squadron (Confirmed and Probable)

Date	Pilot	SN	Origin	Type	Serial	Code	Nb	Cat.
27.04.42	P/O Randall G. **White**	RAF No. 68130	(NFL)/RAF	He111	**N3370**		1.0	P
	P/O Jack R. **Gavegan**	NZ402128	RNZAF					

*Total: **1.00***

Summary of the aircraft lost on Operations - 125 Squadron

Date	Pilot	S/N	Origin	Serial	Code	Fate
25.10.41	Sgt Clive A.G. **Dale**	NZ402170	RNZAF	**T3985**		†
	Sgt John B. **Bayliss**	NZ40600	RNZAF			-

Total: 1

<u>**COMBAT REPORT (PERSONAL)**</u>

<u>**FIGHTER NIGHT.**</u>

IIN42/d17/18

A) R.E.11.

B) J. (Fighter Night).

C) 27/4/42.

D) "B" Flight, 125 (Newfoundland) Squadron.

E) One.

F) He.111

G) Q215 hrs.

H) West of Bath.

J) 4,500 ft.

K) One probably destroyed. (See claim attached).

L) Nil.

M) Nil.

N) 1. None.
   2. No direct help.

P) a: 50 ft.
   b: Two bursts. First of 2 seconds. Second of two and a half
                                seconds.

R) Took off from Colerne at 0140 hrs.
   Landed at Colerne at 0315 hrs.

On the night of the 27th April, I was ordered to scramble on a "Fighter Night" over Bath at 2,500 ft. After orbiting for a time at this height, I saw tracer from an e/a above and behind me. I then saw the silhouette of an e/a against a background of light cloud. E/a was at that moment approximately 2000 ft above me, crossing my tail at right angles from port to starboard, and was flying into the moon.

I climbed up on his port side, so as to keep him silhouetted against the moon, and obtained a perfect view of what my gunner and myself positively identified as an He.111. The port exhaust flame from both engines was clearly visible, and the moon shining through the perspex of e/a left no doubt whatever as to its type.

E/a began weaving and changing height as I closed in, and when we were approximately 500 to 600 yds away, the tail gunner of the He.111 opened fire on us with tracer from a single m/g. He fired three bursts in all as we closed in, the last burst being outside the angle of his tail gun. The shooting appeared to be of poor quality.

When approximately 50 ft from e/a's port wing, my gunner opened fire from starboard as e/a started diving away to starboard. Our first burst (as already stated) was of 2 seconds' duration approximately, and strikes were observed on e/a's port wing root. Pieces came away from e/a, but no flashes were seen. My gunner fired on about 5 to 10 degrees elevation, with no deflection whatever.

Combat Report (Continued)
————————————————————————

I followed e/a into a starboard turn, after which it turned port and levelled out. My gunner then gave it a 2½ second burst, and further strikes were observed all along bottom of e/a's fuselage which began to glow brightly, between wing root and tail. Large pieces were seen to break off.

Our height was then 1,500 ft, and e/a's speed must have been approximately 200 I.A.S. as we were overhauling it quite easily with 220 to 240 showing on the clock.

E/a then dived very steeply to port, passing under us and returning fire with his dorsal gun. Red tracer was used, and volume of return fire appeared on this occasion to be heavier. It probably came from twin guns.

E/a was then down-moon from me and I lost sight of him.

I turned hard to port in an effort to regain contact and dived after him, down to about 300 or 400 ft, but did not see him again.

We were then about 20 miles South West of Bath, and resumed patrol.

On landing at Colerne, my port oleo leg collapsed for no apparent reason, and a/c slewed round, damaging its port wing-tip and flaps. The port wheel snapped off, but my gunner and myself were unhurt.
A/c Cat. AC.

No cine-gun was used as none was fitted to this a/c.

PILOT'S PERSONAL CLAIM.

In view of the foregoing, one He.111 is claimed as probably destroyed.

Signed....................
     P/O. R. White. Pilot.

Signed....................
     P/O. J. Cavegan, Gunner.

29th April, 1942.

Report rendered by F/O. J.C.F.G. Bentley,
Intelligence Officer, 125 (Newfoundland) Squadron.

Date	Pilot	S/N	Origin	Serial	Code	Fate
16.08.41	Sgt Harold L. **LEARNING**	RAF No. 798566	(NFL)/RAF	**N3499**		†
	-	-				-
19.08.41	Sgt Richard **BASTOW**	RAF No. 1184466	RAF	**T4110**		-
	Sgt Alfred G. **DAVIS**	RAF No. 751697	RAF			-
30.09.41	Sgt Allan G. **OLLEY**	RAF No. 1182344	RAF	**N1681**		-
	Sgt Peter **TEMPLE**	RAF No. 1019204	RAF			-
21.10.41	Sgt George W. **WALTERS**	AUS. 400744	RAAF	**T4104**		-
	Lt **CARRUTHERS***	-	*Army*			-
22.10.41	Sgt Edward J. **HARRINGTON**	RAF No. 930643	RAF	**T4040**		-
	Sgt Robert T. **AITCHISON**	NZ402100	RNZAF			-

Total: 5

**Passenger*

'Ran' White shaking hands to the Hon. Lewis E. Emerson, the Commissioner of Defense of the Government of Newfoundland in October 1942. In the previous April, White with his gunner had made one of the last claims on Defiant of the war. Soon after, White ended his first tour with the 125, but would return for a second tour and ended the war as A Flight CO of No. 125 Squadron.

No. 153 Squadron (code TB):

Number 153 Squadron was formed on 14 October 1941 from A Flight of No. 256 Squadron which arrived at Ballyhalbert, west of Belfast, Northern Ireland, the same day with the advance party. The first Defiants were loaned from 256 and would be officially handed over on 31 October (N3367, N3435, N3440, N3454, T4001 and T4004). Forming up continued during the month with more machines and personnel arriving and would continue well into November as the squadron built to full strength. The first CO, S/L John E.J. Sing, arrived on the last day of October to take command. He was a very experienced pilot, being a Battle of Britain veteran with No. 213 Squadron and eight confirmed victories (one shared) and a DFC to his credit. In the meantime, flown by already operational personnel, the first patrol was carried out on the 22nd by P/O A.C. McKinnon and his gunner Sgt W.B. Mulligan in Defiant N1647. Two nights later, two more patrols were flown, both by N3454 but with a different crew each time. No further patrols were carried out until the end of the month, but various day and night training flights were performed for a total of fifty hours.

In November, little operational flying was achieved, only four patrols, two on the 1st and two on the 25th, but 300 hours or so of day and night training sorties were flown. However, two major accidents occurred during the month that, sadly, resulted in the first aircrew fatalities The first occurred on 13 November when V1175 crashed on landing at Squires Gates, killing the pilot (P/O B.B.H. Best) and injuring the air gunner (Sgt J. Bentley). The second was six days later when N1645 undershot on landing. Again, the pilot (P/O F.H. Anderson) was killed and the air gunner (Sgt G. Humphreys) injured. The next month, the first Blenheim arrived, signifying that the conversion to the Beaufighter was about to get underway. December, compared to the previous months, could be seen as 'busy' with thirteen operational flights recorded, including three on the night of 21/22 December, but no interceptions were made. Seven day patrols were carried out on 31 December in the afternoon. Also, 375 hours of training were flown making for a relatively hectic end to the year. In January 1942, little operational activity was recorded with four patrols on the 10th lifting off at around 22.30. Unfortunately, one of the Defiants never came back. The crew of T3931/TB-E was posted missing about half an hour after take off and it was presumed they had ditched into the sea. Later that month, while taking off for a training flight from Eglinton, Defiant N1647 stalled killing both in board (Sgt Lindeman, RAAF, and Sgt Low RAF). Two replacement Defiants arrived the next day (T3916 and V1178), but the first Beaufighter arrived on the 29th along with some radar observers. Generally speaking, January was mainly dedicated to practice with about 230 hours flown. No operations were carried out in February and March 1942 while more Beaufighters were taken on charge. However, training or flight tests continued and, during a flight test on 18 February, T3914 spun into the sea off Antrim and the two crewmen were killed (F/Sgt J.R. Lucas, RCAF, and F/Sgt C.T. Deane). They would be the last losses sustained by the squadron while equipped with the Defiant. In April, 153 was almost fully operational as a Beaufighter unit and the days of the Defiants were numbered. Nonetheless, a final patrol was carried out on the 25th between 23.30 and 23.59 by F/L Keep and Sgt Pope, but they returned with nothing to report. In May, the Beaufighters took over all operational activity and the last Defiant left. In all, the squadron flew just 25 operational patrols with their turret fighters.

Summary of the aircraft lost on Operations - 153 Squadron

Date	Pilot	S/N	Origin	Serial	Code	Fate
10.01.42	Sgt Robert W. **FOREMAN**	RAF No. 1052298	RAF	**T3931**	TB-E	†
	Sgt Ralph H.J. **WINTER**	RAF No. 1386870	RAF			†

Total: 1

Date	Pilot	S/N	Origin	Serial	Code	Fate
13.11.41	P/O Brian B.H. **Best**	RAF No. 68763	RAF	**V1175**		†
	Sgt John P. **Bentley**	RAF No. 1262846	RAF			-
19.11.41	P/O Frederick H. **Anderson**	NZ404880	RNZAF	**N1645**		†
	Sgt George D.L. **Humphreys**	RAF No. 1379070	RAF			-
25.01.42	Sgt Ross W. **Lindeman**	Aus. 403141	RAAF	**N1647**	TB-D	†
	Sgt Robert **Low**	RAF No. 817273	RAF			†
18.02.42	F/Sgt John R. **Lucas**	Can./ R.78281	RCAF	**T3914**	TB-A	†
	F/Sgt Cecil T. **Deane**	RAF No. 904963	RAF			†

Total: 4

No. 255 Squadron (code YD):

Formed as the fourth Defiant squadron at Kirton-in-Lindsey (between Hull and Sheffield), within a few days No. 255 Squadron had received its first eight Defiants (N1625, N1629, N3312/YD-T, N3321, N3323, N3333/YD-B, N3334 and N3335) and its first CO, S/L Rodderick L. Smith, who had served with No. 151 Squadron during the Battle of Britain, had arrived. In December, the squadron continued to form up with the arrival of ten more Defiants in two days (8th - L7012, L7036, N1687, N3318, N3378, and 9th - N1727, N3306, N3329, N3340, N3364). Around Christmas, the last batch of fourteen air gunners arrived to bring the squadron to its full complement. Training was conducted rapidly and 255 was operational by the beginning of the new year. The first patrol was carried out on 8 January by F/L Richard M. Trousdale and Sgt F.W.J. Chunn (RNZAF) in N3378, with nothing to report after one hour and 15 minutes of flight. Trousdale was a New Zealander serving in the RAF and had fought in the Battle of Britain with No. 266 Squadron. Four night patrols were detailed over the next few nights and, on the

Richard Trousdale (middle) was a New Zealander serving in the RAF who started the war with 266 Sqn in November 1939 upon completing his training. He fought over Dunkirk, and made his first claims, then participated in the Battle of Britain at the end of which he was posted to 255 Sqn as B flight commander and claimed the first success of the squadron in February 1941. Rested in July, he would return to operations with 409 (RCAF) Sqn in October, flying Beaufighters, and made his final claim there to bring his score to eight confirmed (one shared), three probables and one damaged. In July 1942, he was given command of 488 (NZ) Sqn, another night fighter unit, and remained in that role until February 1943. He is seen here, while CO of 488, with his two flight commanders, S/L Paul Rabone (left) and S/L John Gard'ner, two New Zealanders who also flew Defiants (96 and 141 Sqn respectively). No further operational postings followed when he left 488 and he ended the war with a DFC and Bar. He was killed in an accident on 16 May 1947 while on board a Mosquito.

(via Andrew Thomas)

Defiant N3333 was among the first to be issued to the squadron and became YD-B. It was lost the following May during a patrol. This Defiant is still painted in the Day Fighter Scheme, but that would be quickly changed. *(Andrew Thomas)*

15th, F/L Trousdale and Sgt Chunn were sent to intercept an enemy aircraft. They both sighted a Do17 flying at 12,000 feet travelling in the opposite direction and about 500 feet above them. Trousdale gave chase, but eventually lost the German bomber in the dark before getting within range. In February, the squadron always had two pilots on readiness with a third in reserve and, in all, 42 sorties were flown for the month. During this time, 255 opened its score. On the night of the 10th, enemy aircraft were reported in the area and two interceptions were made. Trousdale and Chunn sighted another aircraft and closed in at 200 yards. Chunn fired three bursts, but the He111 disappeared steeply diving at 100 feet and it was claimed as probable. With the award of the DFC that month, it had been a very good month for Trousdale. In the meantime, Pilot Officer Hall and Sgt H.D.F. Fitzsimons (RNZAF) sighted a He111 and were able to close to a range where Fitzsimons fired three bursts while the German bomber was trying to escape in a dive. The last attack was delivered at 3,500 feet and the He111 was last seen diving towards the sea. It was also claimed as a probable. However, after this initial success, Hall would have something different to talk about less than one week later. On the 16th he took off (N3334) at 00.50 with Fitzsimons to patrol when, after one hour and 25 minutes, he was ordered to return to base. While landing, he overshot the flarepath and crashed. The crew escaped injury but the aircraft had to be repaired out of the squadron facilities; N3340 would later serve in second line units. Taking off for another patrol two hours later, Hall returned to base a couple of minutes later to overshoot once more and collide with another Defiant (N1727). Again, the crew escaped injury, but the Defiant was later declared beyond economical repair. Two accidents in two hours would not look good on Hall's file! Aside from this operational activity, training continued and it was during such a flight that 255 had to report its first fatality early in the month when, in the early afternoon of the 2nd, N3306 stalled while turning final and crashed. The pilot, Sgt A.R. Jacobs, was killed, but the air gunner survived and would return to the squadron after a couple of days spent at the hospital.

Air activity increased in March as the Germans increased their flights over the British Isles. Flight Lieutenant James G. Sanders DFC, shortly after midnight on the 13th, engaged a He111 west of the aerodrome. His gunner, Sgt Hill, was able to fire five bursts from close range. However, the Heinkel was only claimed as a probable. It was a good start for Sanders with the squadron. He was a Battle of Britain veteran from 615 Squadron and had been posted in earlier during the month. The same night, Pilot Officer Wright made an emergency landing in N1770 after a hydraulic leak. The aircraft was later repaired. The next night, the squadron made another claim, a Do17 damaged by Pilot Officer M.F. Wynne-Wilson and Sgt H. Plant. Two hours later, a German intruder aircraft followed Sgts A.R. Smith and H.A. Mackenzie as they were about to land, but fortunately the two long bursts fired by the German aircraft missed the Defiant. From the 21st, a few Hurricanes were taken on charge to be used in conjunction with the Defiants. In April, the squadron was more active than in March with eighty sorties flown. Flight Lieutenant Sanders and his gunner added a damaged Ju88 on the 7/8th and Sgts J. Craig and C.S. Emery (RNZAF) added another German bomber on the night of the 10/11th. Other contacts were made that month, but proved inconclusive. In May, 255 would carry out its highest number of sorties (120). That came about because of

Defiant N3340 was issued a couple of days after N3333 and it is seen here in the standard colours for night fighter operations. It would leave the squadron very early in February for repairs, after being hit on the ground by a Spitfire, and was never issued again to an operational unit. Serving with various AOS or AGS, N3340 was eventually struck off charge after a major accident on April 1943. *(Andrew Thomas)*

new standing orders. The squadron maintained one flight at readiness and one flight available at dusk and one flight at readiness and one flight at thirty minutes available at dawn. The month started badly when P/O Ballantine and his gunner had to bail out of N3333 after the engine exploded during a night patrol. Over the following days, the Luftwaffe intensified its night raids even though the mass movement of units to the future Russian front had already commenced. Many claims were made in May. First, Squadron Leader Smith and Pilot Officer Farnes claimed a Ju88 destroyed on the night of 4/5 May and two nights later Sgt Craig and Sgt Mair claimed a He111 as damaged (and this only because the guns jammed after the first burst). The next night, a He111 was shot down by Sgt Johnson and Sgt Aitchison. The best night came on 9/10 May when four He111s and one Ju88 were claimed as destroyed and all this without counting the claims made by the Hurricanes in that period (one He111 destroyed and two more damaged). Mid-May, the squadron moved to a new aerodrome, Hibaldstow, a few miles from Kirton-in-Linsdey, but the personnel weren't greatly impressed as the new aerodrome's buildings were not finished. The rest of the month was uneventful. In the beginning of June, the new CO, S/L J.S. Bartlett arrived to take over the squadron. He was a former bomber pilot who had been awarded the DFC the previous November and would fly as a supernumerary until the 13th. The arrival of Bartlett was important as he had experience on twin-engine aircraft. The squadron was to be the second unit to convert to the Beaufighter Mk.II. For this task, the first ubiquitous Blenheim dual-control aircraft arrived on the 16th. Operational flights continued as usual and three minor incidents occurred that month. The first was on the 13th and the second three days later (N3316 and N3324 respectively) The last was on the 22nd (N3309) and, like the other two, the aircraft and crew escaped relatively unscathed. June was about to end without anything to report when, on the night of the 24/25th, Sgt Kendal and his New Zealander air gunner Sgt Emery obtained a visual contact at 10,000 feet, identified as an He111, and opened fire on the starboard side from about 100 yards. Hits were registered and two of the German crew were seen to bail out. The Heinkel took evasive action by diving away and Kendall followed down to 8,000 feet and had closed to 25 yards when Emery fired several long bursts. The Heinkel was mortally hit and was seen diving almost vertically, obviously out of control. It was claimed as destroyed. This claim would be the only one in close to 100 sorties. Operations continued with the Defiants in July, but the conversion to the new aircraft was progressing. Two more dual Blenheims were taken on charge and the first two Beaufighter Mk.IIs arrived on the 22nd. Ten were received before the end of July. However, the squadron was able to maintain a high rate of sorties, close to 100, and one He111 was claimed as damaged by Sgt Cox and Sgt Fitzsimons on the 10/11th. In the first week of August, eight more Beaufighters arrived, bringing the number to the standard complement, and extensive training was carried out, but not without the loss of the recently promoted W/C Bartlett who was killed in a flying accident on the 22nd. He was replaced by W/C C.M. Windsor from No. 219 Squadron. The squadron became non-operational on the 23rd. From the beginning of August, the squadron had flown 45 sorties, the last being flown on the 22/23rd, making for a grand total of 553 sorties flown on Defiants. While training on Defiants was stopped at the same time, which would be logical, routine and liaison flights were still logged by the type. It was during one such flight between Turnhouse and Hibaldstow that N3378 crashed on the 29th when it hit a hill in low cloud. Both crewmen were killed (P/O J. Craig, recently commissioned, and AC1 George D. Hempstead, a groundcrewman from the squadron). The last Defiant finally left the squadron early in September.

Claims - 255 Squadron (Confirmed and Probable)

Date	Pilot	SN	Origin	Type	Serial	Code	Nb	Cat.
10.02.41	F/L Richard M. **Trousdale**	RAF No. 42163	(NZ)/RAF	He111	**N1770**		1.0	P
	Sgt Francis W.J. **Chunn**	NZ40733	RNZAF					
	P/O Roger M.D. **Hall**	RAF No. 43009	RAF	He111	**N3335**		1.0	P
	Sgt Harold D.J. **Fitzsimons**	NZ39097	RNZAF					
13.03.41	F/L James G. **Sanders**	RAF No. 37510	RAF	He111	**N1765**		1.0	P
	Sgt Charles R. **Hill**	RAF No. 745903	RAF					
05.05.41	S/L Roderick L. **Smith**	RAF No. 37129	RAF	Ju88	**N3378**		1.0	C
	P/O Eric **Farnes**	RAF No. 77374	RAF					
08.05.41	Sgt Stanley J. **Johnson**	RAF No. 754519	RAF	He111	**N1617**		1.0	C
	Sgt Robert T. **Aitchison**	NZ402100	RNZAF					
09.05.41	P/O Michael F. **Wynne-Wilson**	RAF No. 89625	RAF	He111	**N3364**		1.0	C
	Sgt Harold **Plant**	RAF No. 535172	RAF					
	F/L Richard M. **Trousdale**	RAF No. 42163	(NZ)/RAF	He111	**N3378**		2.0	C
	Sgt Francis W.J. **Chunn**	NZ40733	RNZAF					
	P/O John D. **Wright**	RAF No. 89594	RAF	Ju88	**N3335**		1.0	C
	Sgt Robert I. **McChesney**	NZ40194	RNZAF					
	P/O Hugh G.S. **Wyrill**	RAF No. 89626	RAF	He111	**N3316**		1.0	C
	Sgt Norman H. **Maul**	NZ402114	RNZAF					
25.06.41	Sgt Philip S. **Kendall**	RAF No. 785014	RAF	He111	**N3364**		1.0	C
	Sgt Clifford S. **Enemy**	NZ40204	RNZAF					

Total: 11.00

Summary of the aircraft lost on Operations - 255 Squadron

Date	Pilot	S/N	Origin	Serial	Code	Fate
16.02.41	P/O Roger M.D. **Hall**	RAF No. 43009	RAF	**N3334**		-
	Sgt Harold D.J. **Fitzsimons**	NZ39097	RNZAF			-
04.05.41	P/O Arthur A. **Ballantine**	RAF No. 85650	RAF	**N3333**		-
	Sgt Chrys H.G. **McTaggart**	RAF No. 902423	RAF			-

Total: 2

Date	Pilot	S/N	Origin	Serial	Code	Fate
02.02.41	Sgt Alan R. **Jacobs**	RAF No. 748209	RAF	**N3306**		†
	Sgt Peroy V. **Thornton**	RAF No. 935568	RAF			-
29.08.41	P/O James **Craig**	RAF No. 45843	RAF	**N3378**		†
	AC1 George D. **Hempstead**	RAF No. 1103778	RAF			†

Total: 2

No. 256 Squadron (code JT):

Formed the same day as 255 Squadron, No. 256 Squadron began life at Catterick, half way between Newcastle and Leeds. Aircraft and personnel arrived progressively until the end of the year and the CO, S/L G.H. Gatheral, arrived on 28 December, temporary command being given to F/O J.C. Ford, the Adjutant, in the meantime. The first four Defiants (N1618, N1619, N1697 and N1698), all brand new, were taken on charge on 25 November and were followed by N1648, N1650, N1689 and N1691 the next day. Early in January, the squadron moved to Pembrey, a bit north of Swansea by the Irish Sea, where training continued. Aircraft continued to arrive in January and February 1941. Working-up was slow because of a lack of personnel, like wireless and electrical ground crew, and the squadron would only be more or less complete by mid-February. The squadron then exchanged its initial Defiants for aircraft equipped with VHF and IFF equipment (more suitable for night operations). So far, the squadron had not suffered any major incident, but this happy time ended on the 20th when N3446 crashed during night flying practice and Sergeant Rees who was flying alone was killed. The same thing happened to N3520 a few days later due to a shortage of petrol. The pilot Sidney Johnson, one of the two flight commanders, but this time the air gunner, Sgt Lewis was able to bail out. Both have been recently posted from No. 600 Sqn. More casualties followed in March. On the 12th Sgt John Hocknell, and S/L Robert Traill, a passenger from HQ No. 10 Group, were killed when Hocknell lost control in cloud and dived into a hillside. The same day, the squadron at last became operational with four aircraft on standby for operations each night. No patrols would be flown from Pembrey, the squadron receiving orders to move to Squires Gate near Blackpool. With the move completed, 256 was able to detail its first three patrols on the night of 30/31 March. All were uneventful. The same month, the squadron's inventory was completed with the addition of a handful of Hurricanes.

'Jumbo' Deanesly participated in the Battle of Britain, flying Spitfires, with 152 Sqn. He joined 256 in January 1941 where he made four confirmed claims to become the most successful pilot of the squadron's time on Defiants. A DFC followed. He later commanded the squadron, holding this position until April 1942. He later served in the Middle East and ended the war at the head of the Dakota equipped 575 Sqn.
While with 256, he was teamed with Sgt William Scott, a New Zealander. Scott completed his tour in May 1942 with a DFM. In March 1943 he was involved in an aircraft accident and suffered a fractured spine. He returned to New Zealand and was eventually discharged in October 1944.

Defiant N1744 during a daytime training flight in 1941. This Defiant was part of the 256 Sqn inventory between February and September 1941. It, like many others, was converted for target-towing duties, but was never allocated to any unit in this configuration before being finally struck off charge in October 1945. *(Andrew Thomas)*

The squadron really entered the war in April. Between the 6th and the 10th, more than forty patrols were carried out during which a Ju88 and a He111 were claimed as destroyed by F/L D.R. West and Sgt R. Adams and F/L E.C. Deanesly and Sgt Scott (RNZAF) respectively. However, these first two claims were countered by the loss of two Defiants. N1694, flown by F/Sgt J. Stenton and Sgt W. Ross, suffered a radio equipment failure during a patrol and, after running out of fuel, was abandoned in flight. A few hours later, the squadron lost the second Defiant during a training flight. Sadly, the crew perished. Misfortune continued as, on the 11th, while on patrol, the crew of N3460 became lost in bad weather and bailed out. Due to less German activity than previous months, only a few patrols were carried out to bring the total for the month to 68.

In early May, the Germans were very active over Liverpool, Warrington and Preston. Flight Lieutenant E.C. Deanesly and his gunner, Sgt W.J. Scott (RNZAF), shot down a Do17 and probably destroyed a Ju88 on the night of 3/4 May (the latter was confirmed afterwards). The same crew shot down a He111 on the night of the 7/8th while F/L D.R. West, with Sgt R.T. Adams, and P/O D. Toone, with P/O R.L. Lamb, claimed one each. One He111 and two Ju88s were also claimed as damaged, but the gunners of one of the latter hit N3500's glycol tank. The cockpit was soon filled with fumes and liquid and the crew, S/L G.H. Gatheral and F/O D.S. Wallen, bailed out safely. These actions would lead to the award of the DFC for Deanesly and the DFM for Scott. The squadron lost another Defiant a few days later when T3955 crashed during a training flight killing Sgt P.J. Taylor and F.R. Fremlin (RNZAF).

In the next three months, operational activity dropped drastically, with 39, 24 and eight night patrols carried out respectively. The Luftwaffe had indeed left for other skies, the invasion of the Soviet Union, so the night raids were few and far between. A couple of German bombers were seen but no interceptions were made. On the other side, the squadron lost three Defiants during that period, all in August. The first loss occurred on the 18th when P/O N.J. Sharpe was badly injured when he crashed into a hill during a night practice flight while flying alone. He was found the next day around midnight but, although taken to hospital, he died later in the day. On the 27th a fatal air collision over Blackpool station occurred between a Botha (L6509) and a Defiant from the squadron. The Kiwi Defiant crew was killed along with the three airmen on board the Botha which crashed onto the Booking Hall and burst into flames killing a further fourteen on the ground. The squadron's air gunner, Sgt N.A. Clifford (RNZAF) had tried to bail out but was too low and his chute did not open in time. Then, four days later, it was the turn of N1770 to encounter

Another view of N1744/JT-S in flight.

Defiant T4037 flew with 256 Sqn between October 1941 and May 1942 when it was passed to 287 Sqn, an ASR unit. It was later converted to a TT.III for target-towing duties.

engine trouble and a crash landing on a beach followed. The pilot, P/O F.T. Reynolds, was injured, but the air gunner, F/Sgt E.C. Smith, who had bailed out, was safe.

September was a very quiet month with only seven sorties recorded. Flight Lieutenant Deanesly took over the squadron from the 1st. Until the end of the year, 256 saw little air activity with a peak in October of 29 sorties during which a Ju88 was claimed as destroyed by F/L Coleman and Sgt Smith during the last hours of the 22nd. T3998 overshot on landing while returning from a patrol and was badly damaged. The Defiant would be struck off charge four days later. The crew were not injured. However, Sgt E. Williams would have less luck on 4 November when, during a training flight, T4053's engine failed obliging the crew to bail out. Williams landed in the sea and drowned, but the pilot was unhurt. If the end of 1941 was marked by a lack of operational activity, the first months of 1942 were worse with only thirteen sorties flown until the end of May, the squadron now slated to convert to the Beaufighter. In spring, the first Defiant Mk.II arrived, but less than ten would eventually serve with the unit. That did not prevent accidents, however. V1116 crashed into the sea off Lytham Pier on 7 February while simulating attacks on coastal battery. Both crew were killed as was the crew of T3995

Defiant N1770/JT-U seen before it was lost during a night patrol in the early hours of 1 September 1941.

which stalled on approach and crashed. However, the crew of T3946 was luckier on the 11th when they bailed out safely after the undercarriage jammed and would not lower. The only real action occurred on the 29th when P/O Jones and Sgt Robinson were sent to intercept an enemy aircraft, but did not see it. However, another enemy aircraft saw them and opened fire. Fortunately, no damage was caused. In May, the first Beaufighter arrived at the squadron, the Defiant now regarded as totally obsolete for the role. A final sortie was carried out on the 27th when Sgt D.K. Cotterill and Sgt R. Craig patrolled at 16,000 feet without making any interceptions. A few days later, the squadron moved to Woodvale, near Liverpool, and left its Defiants behind. In all, 256 flew 300 sorties with the Defiant.

Claims - 256 Squadron (Confirmed and Probable)

Date	Pilot	SN	Origin	Type	Serial	Code	Nb	Cat.
10.02.41	F/L Donal R. **WEST**	RAF No. 42087	RAF	Ju88	**N3445**	JT-F	1.0	C
	Sgt Reginald T. **ADAMS**	RAF No. 759300	RAF					
10.04.41	F/L Edward C. **DEANESLY**	AAF No. 90251	RAF	He111	**N1770**	JT-U	1.0	C
	Sgt William J. **SCOTT**	NZ40283	RNZAF					
03.05.41	F/L Edward C. **DEANESLY**	AAF No. 90251	RAF	Do17	**N3450**	JT-N	1.0	C
	Sgt William J. **SCOTT**	NZ40283	RNZAF					
				Ju88			1.0	C
08.05.41	P/O Donavan **TOONE**	RAF No. 86672	RAF	He111	**T3984**	JT-H	1.0	C
	F/O Robert L. **LAMB**	RAF No. 82718	RAF					
	F/L Donal R. **WEST**	RAF No. 42087	RAF	He111	**N3445**	JT-F	1.0	C
	Sgt Reginald T. **ADAMS**	RAF No. 759300	RAF					
	F/L Edward C. **DEANESLY**	AAF No. 90251	RAF	He111	**N1745**	JT-P	1.0	C
	Sgt William J. **SCOTT**	NZ40283	RNZAF					
22.10.41	F/L George B.S. **COLEMAN**	RAF No. 28146	RAF	He111	**T3995**	JT-U	1.0	C
	F/Sgt Godfrey E. **SMITH**	RAF No. 969504	RAF					

Total: 8.00

Summary of the aircraft lost on Operations - 256 Squadron

Date	Pilot	S/N	Origin	Serial	Code	Fate
16.02.41	F/Sgt John **STENTON**	RAF No. 514976	RAF	**N1694**	JT-K	-
	Sgt William **ROSS**	RAF No. 759030	RAF			-
11.04.41	Sgt Ronald **DEAN**	RAF No. 937266	RAF	**N3460**	JT-G	-
	Sgt Reginald L. **ROBINSON**	NZ402116	RNZAF			-
08.05.41	S/L George H. **GATHERAL**	RAF No. 34134	RAF	**N3500**	JT-B	-
	F/O Dennis S. **WALLEN**	RAF No. 77347	RAF			-
01.09.41	P/O Frederick T. **REYNOLDS**	RAF No. 86373	RAF	**N1770**	JT-U	-
	F/Sgt Eric C. **SMITH**	AAF No. 800636	RAF			-

Total: 4

Date	Pilot	S/N	Origin	Serial	Code	Fate
20.02.41	Sgt David K. **Rees**	RAF No. 748248	RAF	**N3446**		†
	-		-			-
26.02.41	F/L Sidney F.F. **Johnson**	AAF No. 91005	RAF	**N3520**		†
	Sgt Charles S. **Lewis**	RAF No. 801451	RAF			-
12.03.41	Sgt John **Hocknell**	RAF No. 748123	RAF	**N3451**		†
	S/L Robert A.E. **Traill**	RAF No. 36018	RAF			†
08.04.41	Sgt John D.H. **Cunningham**	RAF No. 923918	RAF	**N3424**		†
	Sgt Albert D. **Wood**	NZ401819	RNZAF			†
15.05.41	Sgt Peter J. **Taylor**	RAF No. 958721	RAF	**T3955**	JT-R	†
	Sgt Erle R. **Fremlin**	NZ402108	RNZAF			†
18.08.41	P/O Norman J. **Sharpe**	RAF No. 67097	RAF	**N1651**	JT-Z	†
	-		-			-
27.08.41	Sgt Lincoln J. **Ellmers**	NZ40760	RNZAF	**N1745**	JT-O	†
	Sgt Noel A. J. **Clifford**	NZ402166	RNZAF			†
04.11.41	Sgt Joseph **Berry**	RAF No. 1177137	RAF	**T4053**		-
	Sgt Edward V. **Williams**	RAF No. 746874	RAF			†
07.02.42	P/O William J.P. **Olney**	RAF No. 112509	RAF	**V1116**	JT-H	†
	Sgt Stanley W. **Greenwood**	Aus. 400345	RAAF			†
11.02.42	P/O Henry P. **Harrison-Yates**	RAF No. 10489	RAF	**T3946**		-
	Sgt **Woodford**	?	?			-
26.02.42	Sgt Francis W. **Joyce**	NZ404376	RNZAF	**T3995**	JT-U	†
	Sgt Gordon F. **Walden**	NZ402117	RNZAF			†

Total: 11

Joseph Berry was posted to 256 Sqn from 59 OTU at the end of August 1941. His start was difficult as he had to bail out over the sea when T4053 suffered engine failure during a training flight. Sadly, his air gunner drowned. Berry would eventually achieve an outstanding war career and become the top scorer against the V-1s during the summer of 1944 (sixty destroyed). He ended the war with a DFC and two Bars.

No. 307 (Polish) Squadron (code EW):

This Polish squadron was formed at Kirton-in-Lindsey on 5 September 1940 during the most critical days of the Battle of Britain. It would be the only Polish night fighter squadron in the RAF and, at the same time, the only night fighter unit manned by non-Commonwealth personnel. The squadron was intended to be equipped with Hurricanes, but this plan was quickly dropped and Defiants were chosen instead. The first OC was S/L George C. Tomlinson, arriving from No. 6 OTU. He had previously commanded 17 Squadron until June 1940 and had been awarded the DFC so was therefore a very experienced pilot. The first Polish personnel arrived over the next few days, including S/L S. Pietraszkiewicz, the Polish CO, and the two Polish flight commanders, Flight Lieutenants W. Szcześnieswki and K. Kosinski. Training commenced on the 11th with one Fairey Battle (a second was loaned by the station) and one Miles Master pending the arrival of the Defiants on the 14th (L7035, N1559, N1560, N1636 to N1643 and N1686). On the 16th, the British B Flight commander arrived, F/L Hubert P.F. Ratten, from 64 Squadron. In the next few days, the squadron received its complement of aircraft (N1624, N1671, N1696, N1704 on the 17th; N1675, N1683, N1684, N1695 on the 18th; and N1682 the next day) and F/L Cole, the British A Flight commander, reported to the squadron. However, 307 was facing a major issue at the time as bad communication between the Poles and the British at higher levels made the former think the squadron would be a Hurricane unit so single seat fighter pilots, not two-seater experts, had been posted in. Consequently, the first batch of pilots was soon re-posted, but replacements then had to be waited on. Pending new postings and the arrival of new pilots, the Poles continued to carry out training flights and 200 hours were flown during the last week of September. It was not until the first days of October that the expected change finally occurred when S/L Benz arrived for flying duties. On the 5th, the first accident occurred, but the Defiant (L7035) was repaired on site. The same day, seventeen Polish air gunners reported to the squadron as, so far, only a handful of gunners had arrived. The turnover of the pilots took longer than planned and it was not until the very last days of October that the new pilots began to arrive. During all of October, training continued as far as weather permitted and some days close to thirty hours were flown, but at the expense of the Battle which was damaged on the 30th (R7411). On 2 November, instructions were received to move to Jurby on the Isle of Man. This took place on the 7th and one week later, S/L Benz, the Polish CO, relinquished commend to F/L Grodzicki who was promoted to squadron leader at the same time. November was spent training and one Defiant was damaged on the 26th (N1624), but without major consequences for the aircraft or crew.

In the first days of December, 307 became operational on Defiants, providing a detachment to Cranage and Squires Gate. On the 4th, the squadron maintained a section on readiness all day and continued to do so for several days owing to the weather. Besides this, training continued throughout the month with the same intensity as previous weeks. On 8 December, Red section (L7020/N1683/N1696), led by P/O Buczynski and Sgt Frąckiewicz, took off for a convoy patrol and returned half an hour later with nothing to report. The squadron carried out 39 convoy patrols over the remainder of the month. With training flights, 307 flew about 385 hours on Defiants in December. January 1941 almost repeated December's effort with 35 convoy patrols during the month for a total of about 390 flight hours. However, the squadron began to take on new Defiants equipped with VHF, the first two (N3315 and N3435) arriving on the 6th. On the 10th, after becoming lost on patrol, Defiant N3401 crashed while attempting to ditch off Barmouth, killing Sergeants A. Joda and W. Gandurski. At the end of the month, the squadron moved permanently to Squires Gate. In February, air activity was reduced, mainly because of the bad weather, with 320 hours flown and only six patrols (9th, 15th and 24th) but one Defiant was lost on training during aerobatics, crashing near Eren Green on 10th. Both on board were killed, including Sgt Bochenski who at 41 was one of the oldest operational Polish fighter pilot. A seventh patrol had been planned on 25 February, but, while taking off, N3375 collided with a stationary lorry and AC.1 William W. Short, Petrol Driver, was killed. The Defiant stopped on the side on the runway, both crewmen safe. In March, the squadron was airborne 51 times at night and, for the first time, an encounter with an enemy aircraft occurred. On 12 March, N3439 engaged a He111 over Ruthin and the air gunner fired a burst of three seconds. The gunners of the Heinkel returned fire, but the Defiant was not hit. The results were far from conclusive so the Heinkel was claimed as damaged, the first claim for 307 (Sgt Jankowiak/Sgt Karais). The same night, as the Germans seemed to be active in the area, the detachment at Squires Gate worked in conjunction with three Hurricanes from 229 Squadron. The Germans returned to the sector over the next few days and, on the night of the 14th, N3439 claimed an enemy bomber as probably destroyed at 20,000 feet. The air gunner fired two bursts and both he, Sgt Niewolski, and the pilot, F/O Lewandowski, saw the aircraft hit and dive straight down. A few days later, S/L Tomlinson left the squadron for a HQ position at No. 9 Group so 307 was now commanded by a Pole (S/L Grodzicki). At the end of March, the squadron made another move, this time to Colerne.

The weather during the first week of April was so awful that no patrols could be flown. The crews had to wait until the very early hours of the 7th to get into the air. The next night, Defiant N1809 encountered a Do17 and the air gunner fired two bursts of twenty rounds each after having turned to starboard. No results were seen and the Dornier disappeared into cloud. On 10 April, a dramatic accident occurred when, returning from a R/T flight around 15.20, Defiant N3390 stalled on approach to Colerne while trying to avoid another aircraft and crashed three miles north-east of Bath. The pilot, Sgt M. Frychel, and the air gunner, LAC J. Dziubek were killed. During the night, a He111 was attacked (N3391) but, despite three bursts fired from 200 yards, no results were observed. After many inconclusive encounters, the squadron's luck changed at last in the early hours of the 12th, when Sgt Jankowiak, pilot, and Sgt Lipinski, gunner, in N3315 shot down a He111 discovered 1,500 feet below them. The Poles were patrolling at 15,000 feet. Jankowiak turned to port in a complete circle and descended allowing the gunner to open fire at forty yards into the nose of the Heinkel. Many hits were seen and the He111 dived steeply into cloud and disappeared, the pilot probably being mortally wounded. A crashed Heinkel was later found in the area and the claim confirmed by Fighter Command. During the late evening of the same day, F/L Jakszewicz and Sgt Starosta in N1809 were vectored several times to a Heinkel intruder but, this time, the interception was not successful. Four nights later, F/O Lewandowski and Sgt Zackroki claimed another Heinkel as probably destroyed after a long combat that exhausted their ammunition, but the claim would be downgraded to damage only. The combat was fierce as the German gunners returned fire, but the Heinkel was seen leaving the area losing height with smoke coming from the left engine. The Germans continued to be very active over the next few days, but, despite various attempts at interceptions, no more claims were made until the end of the month. However, the squadron lost another Defiant (N3391), during a patrol on the evening of the 24th, when its engine failed. To avoid a perilous emergency landing at night, the crew decided to abandon the aircraft, and did so safely, before it crashed near Carlton Musgrove. The squadron achieved seventy operational patrols in April and flew about 225 hours. At the end of April, a detachment was sent to Pembrey.

Regarding the number of sorties, May would be the month that would see the highest number, with 101 flown, and the squadron able to get airborne every night of the month bar three. Defiant N1769 took off at 22.50 on 4 May for a routine patrol. It was an unsuccessful patrol, but the Defiant ran out of fuel, after two and a half hours, while returning to land, forcing the crew to bail out over Exeter. A few days later, on the night of the 9th, the aerodrome was bombed by the Germans, but the Poles were unable to make any interceptions. Worse still, two Poles were injured in the bombing. Three nights later, the squadron made its last claim with Defiants

Exeter during the winter of 1940-1941. A mass is celebrated in a hangar while a Defiant with the codes 'EW' of 307 Sqn is parked in front of the entrance. The squadron had just become operational. *(Andrew Thomas)*

A bit blurry, but this photo is interesting as it shows three Defiants of 307 Sqn flying in formation while heading out for a convoy patrol in 1941. The Polish square is clearly visible ahead of the cockpit. The three Defiants are EW-M leading, EW-D on its left, and EW-P on its right.

when Sgt Jan Malinowski (pilot) and Sgt S. Jarzembowski (gunner) reported a He111 as destroyed. The Heinkel was attacked from 300 yards, and twenty feet below, and bullets were seen to enter the centre-section of the fuselage. The bomber dived gradually and the Defiant kept below and closed to forty yards. Jarzembowski fired three more short bursts that hit the aircraft in the nose. The pilot was probably hit as the German bomber turned and dived steeply to the right making a partial half roll on to its back. The Defiant did not follow as another Heinkel showed up 600 yards away. The Poles gave chase, but it dived to sea level and was lost. The Defiant returned to patrol and soon sighted a third Heinkel 500 yards away. It was travelling faster than the Defiant and began to fire at the Poles before it dropped its bombs on the aerodrome and dived to the sea level. On the ground, the Germans scored some hits (close to 500 bombs were dropped on and around the aerodrome) and Defiant N3439 was set on fire and destroyed. After this very special night, the rest of the month remained uneventful.

June was quiet and 63 patrols were performed among 285 hours. This month was rather uneventful, other than the change of command, S/L Antonowicz assuming command with effect 1 June, and the sighting of a single Heinkel on the 19th.

The Defiants on charge in July were N1772, N1788, N1812, N3315, N3330, N3404, N3432, N3437, N3490, T3925, T3946, T3980, T3991, T4001, T4002, T4010, T4058 and V1108. Seventy-six sorties, including some convoy patrols, were flown. More than 450 hours were flown on Defiants, a record for the squadron. On 3 August, 307 was informed it would convert to Beaufighters. Activity was reduced, the first Blenheim for dual conversion (L8438) arrived on 12 August, and the first Beaufighter Mk.IIs followed two days later. The Defiants were airborne only four times in August, two on 13 August and two on 15 August (for a grand total of 445). The last patrols were carried out by N3437 (Sgt Jankowiak/Sgt Karais) and N3330 (Sgt Szempliński/Sgt Ostrowski). Before the month was over, the Defiants were sent to maintenance units in batches, the last being recorded on the 29th.

Claims - 307 Squadron (Confirmed and Probable)

Date	Pilot	SN	Origin	Type	Serial	Code	Nb	Cat.
14.03.41	F/O Maksymilian **Lewandowski**	RAF No. 76819	(POL)/RAF	He111	**N3439**		1.0	P
	Sgt Marian **Niewolski**	PAF No. 780059	PAF					
12.04.41	Sgt Kazimierz **Jankowiak**	PAF No. 704437	PAF	He111	**N3315**	EW-C	1.0	C
	Sgt Józef S. **Lipiński**	PAF No. 780187	PAF					
12.05.41	Sgt Jerzy **Malinowski**	PAF No. 780900	PAF	He111	**N3404**		1.0	C
	Sgt Stanisław **Jarzembowski**	PAF No. 780238	PAF					

Total: 3.00

Date	Pilot	S/N	Origin	Serial	Code	Fate
10.01.41	Sgt Antoni **Joda**	PAF No. 783267	PAF	**N3401**		†
	Sgt Wiktor **Gandurski**	PAF No. 780320	PAF			†
24.04.41	Sgt Witold **Dukszto**	PAF No. 780452	PAF	**N3391**		-
	Sgt Jan **Banyś**	PAF No. 780229	PAF			-
05.05.41	P/O Eugeniusz **Przysiecki**	RAF No. 76635	(POL)/RAF	**N1769**		-
	Sgt Jan **Woźny**	PAF No. 780213	PAF			-
12.05.41	*destroyed in air raid*	-	-	**N3439**	EW-A	-

Total: 4

Date	Pilot	S/N	Origin	Serial	Code	Fate
17.02.41	Sgt Kazimierz **Bocheński**	PAF No. 793643	PAF	**N3314**		†
	Sgt Kazimierz **Frąckiewicz**	PAF No. 780039	PAF			†
10.04.41	Sgt Maksymilian **Frychel**	PAF No. 780532	PAF	**N3390**		†
	LAC Jan Edward **Dziubek**	PAF No. 793811	PAF			†

Total: 2

No. 409 (RCAF) Squadron (code KP):

Formed on 7 June 1941 at Digby, south of Lincoln, as the second RCAF night fighter unit, 409 was first placed under the command of W/C Norman B. Petersen, a regular RCAF officer who arrived at the end of the month. The first Defiants were taken on charge on 6 July and within four days seventeen were on squadron charge (N1765, N3321, N3371, N3396, N3425, N3455, N3515, N3516, T3931, T3932, T3934, T3936, T3937, T3938, T3948, V1178 and AA281) Most were new aircraft delivered directly from MUs. The flight commander positions were given to Flying Officers Handbury and Watson on the 11th who were both promoted to flight lieutenant at the same time. Night training began on the 16th. By the end of the month, the squadron had almost its full complement of men and aircraft and had moved to Coleby Grange between Digby and Lincoln. Progress was satisfactory and close to 500 hours were recorded during the month, including 82 at night. On 3 August, the first operational patrol was recorded when a Defiant flown by F/L Handury, pilot, and Sgt Green, gunner, patrolled over the aerodrome, but no enemy activity was noted. Over the next few days, the remaining air gunners joined 409 and the first pilots were declared fully night operational. On 14 August, shortly after midnight and returning from a night training flight, P/O E. Fenwick, flying T3934, hit trees on approach and crashed. He was injured, but his gunner, Sgt Dickson, was unhurt. The squadron was eventually declared fully operational on 20 August and the same night, F/L Handbury carried out a patrol of two and a half hours. Operational activity remained low in August, with a convoy patrol on 26 August (F/L Handbury and Sgt Sage), but before the month ended the first Beaufighter arrived. On the 28th, nine members of the Russian Military mission visited to inspect the Defiants. In August, 409 flew 758 hours on Defiants including 214 at night. On 3 September, while the conversion to the Beaufighter was just starting, the CO was killed in a flying accident in a Beau and was temporarily replaced by F/L Handbury until the arrival of S/L P.Y. Davout three days later. The squadron focused on training on the new mount, but further operational flying was notched up on Defiants with a scramble on 7 September (P/O Head and Sgt

Because the Defiant was only used for a short time by 409 Sqn, photos are rare for this period. Defiant T3937/KP-S was delivered new to the squadron in July 1941 and was passed on to 153 at the end of October that year.

MacDonald) and a handful of night patrols. By the end of September, 409 had recorded 629 hours of flying, but only thirty hours on Defiants (all operational). The remaining hours were flown on Blenheims to ease the conversion to twin-engine aircraft. The Defiant had already started to leave the squadron as only nine were still on charge by 30 September - N1704, N3396, N3398 (arrived 19 August), N3516, T3931, T3932, T3937, T3947 and AA281. Training flights continued on Defiants and during one such flight at night, F/L F.S. Watson lost control of AA281 and was killed when the aircraft crashed. The air gunner, F/Sgt McKinnon, managed to bail out and survived. Generally speaking, little flying was done on Defiants, the remaining air gunners being posted to No. 410 (RCAF) Squadron, and the last Defiants left in November (mainly transferred to the newly formed 153 Squadron), but one, N1704, remained on the squadron's inventory until January 1942 when it was finally passed on to No. 410 Squadron.

Summary of the aircraft lost by accident - 409 Squadron

Date	Pilot	S/N	Origin	Serial	Code	Fate
14.08.41	P/O Eric **FENWICK**	RAF No. 101481	RAF	**T3934**		-
	Sgt John W. **DICKSON**	CAN./ 355A	RCAF			-
11.10.41	F/L Frederick S. **WATSON**	CAN./ C.1372	RCAF	**AA281**		†
	Sgt Alan G. **MACKINNON**	RAF No. 1387905	RAF			-

Total: 2

Paul Davout served in both the pre-war RAF and RCAF before leaving the service to become a bush pilot. He re-joined the RCAF in June 1940, was re-trained and started a career as a night fighter pilot, with 409 and 410 Sqns, flying Defiants and then Beaufighters. Later on, during a second tour, he would lead 418 Sqn, the only RCAF intruder squadron, and by the end of the war he had reached the rank of group captain and was OC the Canadian 143 Wing. He was released from the RCAF in July with a DSO and DFC. He was among the most efficient of the RCAF wartime fighter leaders.

No. 410 (RCAF) Squadron (code RA)

Number 410 Squadron was formed on 30 June 1941 as the third and last Canadian night fighter squadron. As with 409, its first equipment was the Defiant. The squadron was based at Ayr, south of Glasgow. Command of this new unit was given to S/L Davoud who had just completed his course at No. 60 OTU. Aircraft (N1565, N1613, N1630, N1700, N1731, N3503, N3518, T3929, T4036, T4056, T4120, V1110, V1137, V1183 and AA287) and personnel began to arrive over the next few days, but the first crew began to fly Defiants borrowed from No. 141 Squadron for familiarisation purposes (the 141 was also based at Ayr). During one such flight on 8 July, Sgt B.P. Dawbarn, flying alone, was killed in N1798. He was seen doing some steep turns and it appeared that he lost control at a low height and was seen crashing about one mile from Ayr. It wasn't just Defiants that were loaned. A number of pilots and air gunners also came from 141. Training was quickly done nonetheless and, on 23 July, A Flight became operational and was soon scrambled. V1183, piloted by P/O Lucas, returned after 25 minutes with nothing to report. By the end of the month, the squadron had received its full complement of aircraft and personnel, but only ten pilots were operational both day and night, with thirteen more still limited to daytime ops. The squadron flew 306 hours, 47 of them by night. In August, it provided a detachment at Acklington while its new base became Drem, near Edinburgh. In all, 79 sorties were recorded (patrols and scramble), with nothing to report other than the loss of a Defiant during a training flight at night. N1731 flew into a hill killing the crew. In September, 58 more sorties were flown and S/L Davoud left to take command of No. 409 Squadron, the other Canadian Defiant squadron. Command was given to F/L M. Lipton, one of the flight commanders. In October, the number of sorties dropped to 24 (with 385 hours flown, training included), 22 in November (286 hours flown, training included) and thirty in December (380 hours flown including training). Despite many attempts to intercept, no enemy aircraft were encountered but two Defiants were lost in this period of time. N3385 collided with Spitfire P8248 on landing at Drem and V1137, on 9 December, crashed in bad weather returning from an unsuccessful night interception. It struck trees with its landing gear while flying its approach to Drem. The pilot, F/L Day suffered bad head injuries, but the air gunner, F/Sgt Townsend, escaped major injury. Even in a state of shock, Townsend managed to extract his pilot from the wreck and perform first aid with the kit carried in the Defiant and would later receive the British Empire Medal. As far as the personnel were concerned, 410 was a Canadian unit by name only as, for the aircrew, only fifteen of the 55 postings on 31 December were Canadians. The rest were RAF or RAAF and also two Belgian pilots. For the groundcrew, all were British except for one Canadian and one Belgian. If anyone in the squadron was hoping for things to change, and for there to be more action in 1942, they would have been disappointed as nothing happened. The Defiant remained the squadron's mount until April 1942 when the conversion to the Beaufighter II began. Between January and 28 April 1942, the date of the last Defiant ops, only 63 sorties, and close to 1,000

If we exclude the Poles, non-Commonwealth aircrew flying with an operational Defiant squadron were rare. Among them were two Belgians. Left: Albert G.T. van den Branden, a pre-war reserve NCO military Belgian pilot who was recalled for active duty when war broke out. Arriving in the UK in June 1940, he started his RAF tour with 410 Sqn and would leave in April 1942 for 151 Sqn. However, because of his age, 31 in 1941, he could not really expect to serve in front line single engine squadrons. By October 1943, he was serving as a flying instructor and would survive the war. Right: Alfons-Josef Denys, was still under training when the Germans launched their offensive in May 1940. He completed his training with the RAF and 410 was his first operational posting in July 1941. He then went to 151 Sqn and 1451 Flight where he was killed in an accident while flying a Havoc on 22 October 1941.
(André Bar)

The Defiants had to be ready for any interception even in winter when flying at night was always perilous especially in a single engine aircraft. Here, Defiant V1110/RA-H is seen on the snow during the winter of 1941-1942. This aircraft served with 410 between July 1941 and September 1942. It was passed on to the Royal Navy in January 1944 as a TT.III and returned to the RAF in April 1945.

hours, were performed and no enemy aircraft encountered. Of course, the bad winter weather prevented much flying in January and February and the news came that month that the squadron would finally receive the Beaufighter. On 16 March, the squadron lost two aircrew killed in V1183 while flying low during a non-operational flight. The Defiant stalled at high speed leaving no chance for recovery by the pilot. Later, on 27 March, while on an interception, the pilot of N3364, Sgt F.E. Haines, lost control in thick cloud and ordered his gunner to bail out. However, it seems that Haines never did as he was found dead in his crashed Defiant six miles north-west of Morpeth. In March, Canadianisation began at last and by the end of the month, two thirds of the aircrew were RCAF. Early in April, the first Beaufighters were taken on charge and operations were limited to a handful of sorties (one each on the 1st, 3rd, 25th and 28th). Non-operational flights continued in April and on the 11th, the squadron, which had been very unlucky with the Defiant so far, lost its last one when N3503 was seen to break from low cloud in a dive and strike the water. The aircraft sank rapidly and both pilot and air gunner were killed. The cause of the crash was never determined. The Defiants began to leave the squadron in April, and the process was completed in May, putting an end to the far from glorious Defiant era in the history of 410 Squadron after 277 sorties on the type.

Defiant V1123/RA-R warming its engine before a night patrol at the end of the summer of 1941. This Defiant was part of the squadron's inventory between August 1941 and March 1942. Converted to a TT.III, it survived the war to be struck off charge in October 1945.

Defiant RA-O during a VIP inspection at Drem in September 1941. Below, 410 Defiant crews seen at the same period : Sgt W.A. Du Perrier, pilot, Sgt L.L.J. Farley (†04.06.42 with 218 Sqn), gunner, Sgt D.B. Freeman, pilot and Sgt L. Hall, gunner.

Date	Pilot	S/N	Origin	Serial	Code	Fate
08.12.41	F/L Robert L.F. **Day**	RAF No. 41263	RAF	**V1137**	RA-K	-
	F/Sgt John J.S. **Townsend**	RAF No. 937269	RAF			-
26.03.42	Sgt Frank E. **Haines**	Can./ R.73306	RCAF	**N3364**		†
	Sgt Joseph A.J.G. **Pelletier**	Can./ R.53763	RCAF			-

Total: 2

Not all accidents ended with a write-off. N3508/RA-G suffered a landing gear collapse in January 1942. The aircraft returned to service.
(Andrew Thomas)

Summary of the aircraft lost by accident - 410 Squadron

Date	Pilot	S/N	Origin	Serial	Code	Fate
17.02.41	Sgt Brian P. **Dawbarn**	RAF No. 1254571	RAF	**N1798+**		†
	-					-
30.08.41	Sgt Denis W. **Hall**	RAF No. 1168705	RAF	**N1731**		†
	Sgt Denis G. **Cresswell**	RAF No. 751880	RAF			†
19.11.41	Sgt Douglas **Williams**	Can./ R.70480	RCAF	**N3385**		-
	Sgt Alfred H.B. **Hall**	Can./ R.54121	RCAF			-
16.03.42	P/O Ian B. **Constant**	RAF No. 115407	RAF	**V1183**		†
	P/O William J. **Lewis**	RAF No. 115728	RAF			†
11.04.42	Sgt Roderick G. **Smith**	Can./ R.92555	RCAF	**N3503**		†
	Sgt Alan G. **Mackinnon**	RAF No. 1387905	RAF			†

+Aircraft borrowed from 141 Sqn.

Total: 5

A partial view of a Defiant of 456 Sqn, coded SA-H, and possibly AA282. Posing are Sgt David Clark (gunner) and Sgt Hadderley (pilot).

No. 456 (RAAF) Squadron (code PZ then SA)

This squadron was formed on 30 June 1941 to become the sole RAAF night fighter unit. It was stationed at Valley on the Irish Sea. The aim was to gather as many Australian air and ground crew in the squadron as possible, but that proved to be difficult (at least during the early stages of its existence). However, the first CO was an Australian serving with the RAF and a veteran of the Battle of Britain with No. 65 Squadron, S/L C.G.C Olive. The first Defiants arrived on 2 and 4 July with N1558, N1569, N1647, N1690, N3367, N3496, N3497, T3933, T3940, T3950, T4007, V1175, V1177, AA282, AA283, AA284 and AA285 being issued to the squadron. In July, more personnel arrived, including the two flight commanders, F/L J.S. Hamilton, formerly of No. 256 Squadron, and F/L C.A. Cooke, from No. 312 Squadron. Both were British and very experienced. The training program began, but it did not take long for the first dramatic event to occur. On 21 July, Sergeant A. Brookes, a British pilot, was killed when flying solo in Defiant T3933. Training progressed well in July, despite this setback, with 500 hours flown, mainly in day-time flights (75% of the total hours flown). The air gunners, Australians, began to reach 456 in mid-August with sixteen of them posted in. By the end of the month, twenty pilots were operational with nine air gunners ready for ops. In August, 665 hours were flown, half of them at night. Practice continued in September and a second Defiant was lost on the 4th when P/O Tom Cleary (RAAF), in Defiant V1177, struck trees on approach resulting in a forced landing. The Defiant was written off. That same night, 456 carried out its first two patrols with F/L Cooke and F/O Ritchie in N3497 and Sgt Wild and Sgt House in N1647. No contacts were made. By the end of the month, fourteen more sorties had been flown with nothing to report and, on 30 September, the first two Beaufighter Mk.IIs arrived. This had some consequences for 456 Squadron as some pilots preferred to stay on single-engine aircraft and many of the gunners did not want to change to the radar operator role. In October, two more patrols were flown on 1 October, but that month efforts were concentrated on the new aircraft and one last patrol was flown on the 20th (for a total of nineteen). It was flown by F/O Merrifield and Sgt Skiller in N3477, but they returned with nothing to report. The last Defiant left the squadron in mid-November.

Summary of the aircraft lost by accident - 456 Squadron

Date	Pilot	S/N	Origin	Serial	Code	Fate
21.07.41	Sgt Alan F. **BROOKES**	RAF No. 1166497	RAF	**T3900**		†
	-					-
04.09.41	P/O Thomas **CLEARY**	AUS. 404236	RAAF	**V1177**		-
	-					-

Total: 2

While many second-line units used the Defiant, if we concentrate on the units that were directly linked to day or night fighting activity, only a handful can be found, most being the Operational Training Units. The first of these was No. 5 OTU, formed in March 1940 and received its first Defiants (L6950, the first production aircraft, L6971 and L7032) on 5 June. Three days later, L7023 joined to complete the complement of the Defiant section. On 1 November, No. 5 OTU was re-designated No. 55 OTU and the Defiants were transferred to No. 54 OTU which was formed to train night fighter crews, a mission passed to No. 60 OTU in June 1941. At that time the Defiant was at its peak and 60 OTU was formed with four squadrons and an official establishment of 27 Defiants with nine in reserve (not counting the allocation of other types like Masters and Magisters). This OTU would begin to progressively convert to twin-engine types from autumn 1941 and the Defiants had left by June 1942.

Also, it must be mentioned, the AFDU (Air Fighting Development Unit) used seven Defiants - firstly L6952 and L6955 between August 1939 and December 1939, then N1756 and N1765 between May and July 1941. V1121 was taken on charge in July for tactical trials and served as AF-V until October 1942. Defiant Mk.IIs AA382 and AA400 were used for a short time in September and October 1941, but the mark was so similar to the Mk.I that no new improvement regarding the use of the type in the units could be added. The Fighter Interception Unit (FIU) used a handful too from autumn 1940 onwards with N1811 being on charge in November. Defiant AA301 and Mk.II AA372 were also used until spring 1942, but not necessarily at the same time. Their use was limited however. We could add the Air Gunner Schools, but while they were training gunners for the Defiant units, they continued to fly the type well after its withdrawal from the front lines. They are therefore excluded.

Summary of the aircraft lost by accident - 5 OTU

Date	Pilot	S/N	Origin	Serial	Code	Fate
13.07.40	Sub-Lt V.H. BELLAMY	-	RN	K8320		-
	-					
16.08.40	Sgt John D. GWYNNE	RAF No. 742137	RAF	L7010		†
	Sgt William C. MUNRO	RAF No. 755716	RAF			†

Total: 2

Summary of the aircraft lost by accident - 54 OTU

Date	Pilot	S/N	Origin	Serial	Code	Fate
19.04.41	Sgt Józef MURZYN	RAF No. 780493	PAF	L6973		-
	Sgt Erwin SKANDERA	RAF No. 780711	PAF			†
26.04.41	Sgt Frederick C.E. CROZIER	RAF No. 908262	RAF	N1568		†
	F/Sgt George BELL	RAF No. 802438	RAF			†
17.05.41	Sgt Vernon M. RUSSELL	RAF No. 990448	RAF	N1573		-
	Sgt Reginald COWAN	RAF No. 535102	RAF			†
19.05.41	Sgt Harold A.R. MCBIRNEY	RAF No. 1251122	(IRE)/RAF	N1653		†
	-					-
29.05.41	Sgt Kenneth C. GEMMEL	RAF No. 911890	RAF	N1556		†
	Sgt David A. HEGGIE	RAF No. 1053585	RAF			†

Total: 5

The second prototype, K8620, was issued to 5 OTU for training duties as it was built to production standards. Its career was short as it was lost in a flying accident on 13 July 1940.

Date	Pilot	S/N	Origin	Serial	Code	Fate
19.07.41	Sgt Edward A. **Tennant**	RAF No. 1169271	RAF	**V1140**		-
15.08.41	Sgt Gerald F. **Westoby**	RAF No. 1254338	RAF	**N1692**		†
20.08.41	Sgt Walter C. **Vatcher**	RAF No. 798550	(NFL)/RAF	**V1180**		-
	Sgt J.ames M. **Thomas**	RAF No. 798947	(NFL)/RAF			-
29.08.41	Sgt Anthony D.C. **La Gruta**	Aus. 400179	RAAF	**T4042**		†
05.09.41	P/O Władysław **Błasiński**	PAF P-1040	PAF	**N1679**		†
	Sgt Stanisław **Sadawa**	PAF No. 781291	PAF			†
26.09.41	P/O Robert C. **Colley**	Can./ J.5957	RCAF	**V1138**		†
15.10.41	P/O Raleigh J.B. **Peacocke**	NZ403049	RNZAF	**N1739**		-
	Sgt Lawrence **Healey**	RAF No. 1001585	RAF			-
31.10.41	P/O William P. **Woodward**	Can./ J.5980	RCAF	**T4003**		-
	name of the gunner not reported	?	?			-
09.11.41	Sgt Alfred F. **Eckert**	Can./ R.58697	(US)/RCAF	**T3938**		-
20.11.41	Sgt Anthony B. **Reynolds**	RAF No. 1268575	RAF	**N1738**		-
30.11.41	P/O David J. **McBrien**	RAF No. 108811	RAF	**L6962**		-
08.12.41	Sgt Thomas E. **Tressam**	Can./ R.75814	RCAF	**N1570**		†
	Sgt Charles **Martin**	RAF No. 1127873	RAF			†
11.12.41	Sgt Frank K. **Coates**	Can./ R.84530	RCAF	**N1754**		-
	name of the gunner not reported	?	?			-
30.12.41	Sgt Stephen C. **Rhynas**	RAF No. 778717	(NR)/RAF	**N1680**		-
01.01.42	Sgt Hiram **Wolf**	Can./ R.77476	RCAF	**N3432**		†
02.01.42	Sgt Malcolm M. **MacDonald**	Can./ R.78720	RCAF	**N1797**		-
03.01.42	P/O James A. **McCague**	Can./ J.7435	RCAF	**N1743**		-
04.01.42	P/O Howard G. **Daniel**	Can./ J.7084	RCAF	**N1799**		-
	Sgt William T. **McMillan**	Aus. 403008	RAAF	**N3495**		†
	Sgt Trevor H. **Jones**	RAF No. 1311958	RAF			†
05.01.42	Sgt James H. **Morrison**	Can./ R. 79101	RCAF	**L7032**		-
14.01.42	Sgt Kenneth G. **Drinkwater**	Can./ R. 82160	RCAF	**V1182**		†
	Sgt John H. **Lowry**	RAF No. 1027413	RAF			†
15.01.42	P/O Albert A.W. **Harris**	RAF No. 110951	RAF	**N3422**		†
	Sgt George C. **Townsend**	RAF No. 1305422	RAF			†
29.01.42	Sgt Benjamin M. **Haight**	Can./ R.90510	RCAF	**N7023**		-
08.02.42	Sgt Thomas **Lawrence**	RAF No. 1259147	RAF	**N1705**		†
	Sgt Andrew **Lawrie**	NZ403607	RNZAF			†
26.02.42	Sgt Thomas H. **Hough**	Can./ R.69424		**T4107**		-

| 18.03.42 | Sgt George A.P. **SANDERS** | CAN./ R.91798 | RCAF | **N1629** | - |
| | Sgt Thomas J. **ROBERTS** | RAF No. 1081482 | RAF | | - |

Total: 26

Canadian from Winnipeg (Manitoba), Frederick S. Watson was killed in a flying accident in October while serving No. 409 Sqn, RCAF. He enlisted in November 1939 and was sent in the summer 1940 to the UK to participate to the Battle of Britain, flying with No. 3 Squadron early in October, before being posted to No. 1 (RCAF) Squadron at the end of the same month. He was posted to the 409 on formation in June 1941 and proceeded immediately to No. 60 OTU for instruction on Defiants, returning to the 409 early in August.

IN MEMORIAM

Defiant (day and night fighters)

Name	Service No	Rank	Age	Origin	Date	Serial
ANDERSON, Frederick Hugh	NZ404880	P/O	22	RNZAF	19.11.41	N1645
ANGELL, Walter Barry	RAF No. 916859	Sgt	24	RAF	27.04.41	N3389
ASH, Robert Clifford Vacy	RAF No. 31023	F/L	31	RAF	28.08.40	L7021
ATKINS, Frederick Peter John	RAF No. 903401	Sgt	n/k	RAF	19.07.40	L7015
BAINBRIDGE, William	RAF No. 1378960	Sgt	29	RAF	15.11.41	AA423
BELL, George	RAF No. 802438	F/Sgt	29	RAF	26.04.41	N1568
BERRY, Alan	RAF No. 968035	Sgt	23	RAF	2308.40	L7027
BEST, Brian Bertram Horace	RAF No. 68763	P/O	n/k	RAF	13.11.41	V1175
BLASINSKI, Wladyslaw	PAF P-1040	F/O	24	PAF	05.09.41	N1679
BOCHENSKI, Kazimierz	PAF No. 793643	Sgt	41	PAF	17.02.41	N3314
BROMLEY, John Stuart Mee	RAF No. 521432	LAC	24	RAF	13.05.40	L6958
BROOKES, Alan Fincher	RAF No. 1166497	Sgt	25	RAF	21.07.41	T3900
CLIFFORD, Noel Anthony John	NZ402166	Sgt	23	RNZAF	27.08.41	N1745
CRAIG, James	RAF No. 45843	P/O	n/k	RAF	29.08.41	N3378
CROMBIE, Robert	RAF No. 903506	Sgt	29	RAF	19.07.40	L6974
CROZIER, Frederick CharlesEric	RAF No. 908262	Sgt	20	RAF	26.04.41	N1568
CHANDLER, Gordon Emery	RAF No. 33559	P/O	20	RAF	13.05.40	L6980
COLLEY, Robert Charles	CAN./ J.5957	P/O	22	RCAF	26.09.41	V1138
CONSTANT, Ian Brancovan	RAF No. 115407	P/O	21	RAF	16.03.43	V1183
COOKE, Nicholas Gresham	RAF No. 37652	F/L	26	RAF	31.05.40	L6975
COWAN, Reginald	RAF No. 535102	F/Sgt	25	RAF	17.05.41	N1573
CRESSWELL, Denis George	RAF No. 751880	F/Sgt	23	RAF	30.08.41	N1731
CUNNINGHAM, John Denis Harold	RAF No. 923918	Sgt	21	RAF	08.04.41	N3424
CURLEY, Albert George	RAF No. 747968	Sgt	33	RAF	19.07.40	L6995
DAISLEY, Lionel Charles William	RAF No. 741278	Sgt	n/k	RAF	28.05.40	L6953
DALE, Clive Alan Gillions	NZ402170	Sgt	20	RNZAF	25.10.41	T3985
DAWBARN, Brian Proctor	RAF No. 1254571	Sgt	18	RAF	17.02.41	N1798
DEANE, Cecil Thomas	RAF No. 904963	F/Sgt	25	RAF	18.02.42	T3914

Name	Service No.	Rank	Age	Service	Date	Aircraft
DONALD, Ian David Grahame	RAF No. 33306	F/L	*n/k*	RAF	19.07.40	L7009
DRINKWATER, Kenneth Gordon	CAN./ R. 82160	Sgt	*n/k*	RCAF	14.01.42	V1182
DZIUBEK, Jan Edward	PAF No. 793811	Sgt	26	PAF	10.04.41	N3390
ELLMERS, Lincoln John	NZ40760	Sgt	24	RNZAF	27.08.41	N1745
FIDLER, Alfred	RAF No. 743039	LAC	27	RAF	31.05.40	L6968*
FOREMAN, Robert Wilkinson	RAF No. 1052298	Sgt	*n/k*	RAF	10.01.42	T3931
FRACKIEWICZ, Kazimierz	PAF No. 780039	Sgt	24	PAF	17.02.41	N3314
FREMLIN, Erle Rutherford	NZ402108	Sgt	19	RNZAF	15.05.51	T3955
FRYCHEL, Maksymilian	PAF No. 780532	Sgt	22	PAF	10.04.41	N3390
GANDURSKI, Wiktor	PAF No. 780320	Sgt	25	PAF	10.01.41	N3401
GAZZARD, Royce Victor	RAF No. 744873	Sgt	21	RAF	14.12.41	AA429
GEMMEL, Kenneth Campbell	RAF No. 911890	Sgt	21	RAF	29.05.41	N1556
GODSMARK, Howard Alfred	RAF No. 1255377	Sgt	*n/k*	RAF	12.11.41	AA428
GOLDSMITH, John Ernest	RAF No. 901859	Sgt	19	RAF	27.04.41	N3389
GOODALL, Harold Ingham	RAF No. 79159	P/O	25	RAF	08.10.40	N1627
GORDON-DEAN, Peter Lee	RAF No. 33436	F/O	21	RAF	04.03.41	N1794
GREENWOOD, Stanley Wheatley	AUS. 400345	Sgt	29	RAAF	07.02.42	V1116
GWYNNE, John Draper	RAF No. 742137	Sgt	20	RAF	16.08.40	L7010
HACKWOOD, Gerald Henry	RAF No. 42217	P/O	20	RAF	20.11.40	N1626
HAINES, Frank Ernest	CAN./ R.73306	Sgt	19	RCAF	26.03.42	N3364
HALL, Denis Winton	RAF No. 1168705	Sgt	21	RAF	30.08.41	N1731
HAMILTON, Arthur Charles	RAF No. 78543	P/O	28	RAF	19.07.40	L7009
HARRIS, Albert Andrew William	RAF No. 110951	P/O	20	RAF	15.01.42	N3422
HART, Herbert Wyndham	RAF No. 115127	P/O	*n/k*	RAF	29.03.42	AA384
HATFIELD, Jack Elmer	RAF No. 40474	P/O	28	(CAN)/RAF	28.05.40	L7007
HEGGIE, David Alexander	RAF No. 1053585	Sgt	26	RAF	29.05.41	N1556
HEMPSTEAD, George Daniel	RAF No. 1103778	AC1	27	RAF	29.08.41	N3378
HICKMAN, Guy Lewis	RAF No. 42225	P/O	19	RAF	31.05.40	L6968
HOCKNELL, John	RAF No. 748123	Sgt	21	RAF	12.03.41	N3451
HOWLEY, Richard Alexander	RAF No. 41705	P/O	*n/k*	(NFL)/RAF	19.07.40	L6995
HUNTER, Philip Algernon	RAF No. 32081	S/L	27	RAF	24.08.40	N1535
HUTCHESON, George Anderson	RAF No. 79161	P/O	30	RAF	11.06.40	L6970
JACOBS, Alan R.	RAF No. 748209	Sgt	20	RAF	02.02.41	N3306
JEE, George Victor	RAF No. 1163268	Sgt	21	RAF	15.11.41	AA423
JODA, Antoni	PAF No. 783267	F/Sgt	25	PAF	10.01.41	N3401
JOHNSON, Charles Edward	RAF No. 79241	P/O	35	RAF	28.08.40	L7026
JOHNSON, Sidney Frederick Farquhar	AAF No. 91005	F/L	25	RAF	26.02.41	N3520
JOHNSON, Stanley Bernard	RAF No. 747782	Sgt	37	RAF	31.05.40	L6980
JONES, Evan John	RAF No. 744999	Sgt	31	(CAN)/RAF	29.05.40	L6957*
JONES, Joseph Trevor	RAF No. 78855	P/O	21	RAF	24.08.40	L6966
JONES, Trevor Hartley	RAF No. 1311958	Sgt	19	RAF	04.01.42	N3495
JOYCE, Francis William	NZ404376	Sgt	22	RNZAF	26.02.42	T3995
KEENE, Steven Francis Henry	RAF No. 514292	Sgt	27	RAF	15.05.40	L6991
KELLEY, Lawrence Henry	RAF No. 917145	Sgt	22	RAF	09.03.42	AA403
KENNER, Peter Lewis	RAF No. 73032	P/O	21	RAF	28.08.40	L7026
KEMP, John Richard	RAF No.41850	P/O	25	(NZ)/RAF	19.07.40	L6974
KIDSON, Rudal	RAF No. 41297	P/O	26	(NZ)/RAF	19.07.40	L7015
KING, Frederick Harry	RAF No. 43845	P/O	*n/k*	RAF	24.08.40	N1535
LA GRUTA, Anthony Dominica Cyril	AUS. 400179	Sgt	23	RAAF	29.08.41	T4042
LAWRENCE, Thomas	RAF No. 1259147	Sgt	19	RAF	08.02.42	N1705
LAWRIE, Andrew	NZ403607	Sgt	19	RNZAF	08.02.42	N1705
LEARNING, Harold Lewis	RAF No. 798566	Sgt	22	(NFL)/RAF	16.08.41	N3499
LEWIS, Wallace John	AUS. 404565	F/Sgt	22	RAAF	26.04.42	AA377
LEWIS, William John	RAF No. 115728	P/O	*n/k*	RAF	16.03.42	V1183
LINDEMAN Ross Wellesley	AUS. 403141	Sgt	21	RAAF	25.01.42	N1647
LIPPETT, Albert	RAF No. 348039	Cpl	37	RAF	31.05.40	L6975
LOW, Robert	RAF No. 817273	F/Sgt	26	RAF	25.01.42	N1647
LOWRY, John Havergal	RAF No. 1027413	Sgt	20	RAF	14.01.42	V1182

Name	Service No.	Rank	Age	Force	Date	Aircraft
LUCAS, John Robert	Can./ R.78281	F/Sgt	24	RCAF	18.02.42	T3914
MACHIN, William Harold	RAF No. 968717	Sgt	20	RAF	24.08.40	L6965
MAIR, William	RAF No. 971422	F/Sgt	27	RAF	26.04.42	AA377
MAXWELL, Walter	RAF No. 967872	Sgt	23	RAF	26.08.40	L7025
MACKINNON, Alan Gordon	RAF No. 1387905	Sgt	19	RAF	11.04.42	N3503
MACLEOD, Alexander	RAF No. 42013	P/O	n/k	RAF	28.05.40	L7007
MARTIN, Charles	RAF No. 1127873	Sgt	20	RAF	08.12.41	N1570
McBIRNEY, Harold Albert Rodney	RAF No. 1251122	Sgt	20	(IRE)/RAF	19.05.41	N1653
McLEISH, Douglas Leslie	RAF No. 581467	LAC	20	RAF	13.05.40	L6960
McMILLAN, William Thomas	Aus. 403008	Sgt	23	RAAF	04.01.42	N3495
MILLS, Athony Ian	RAF No. 1160033	Sgt	21	RAF	14.12.41	AA429
MUNRO, William Campbell	RAF No. 755716	Sgt	26	RAF	16.08.40	L7010
O'MALLEY, Derek Keppel Coleridge	RAF No. 72475	F/O	29	RAF	04.09.40	N1628
OLNEY, William John Paterson	RAF No. 112509	P/O	n/k	RAF	07.02.42	V1116
PHILLOTT, Albert Henry	RAF No. 1379505	Sgt	32	RAF	09.03.42	AA403
PLEDGER, Geoffery Frank Coleman	RAF No. 79216	F/O	35	RAF	04.04.41	T3913
PONTING, William Alan	RAF No. 79217	P/O	30	RAF	24.08.40	L6966
RASMUSSEN, Lauritz Andrew Rodney	NZ391868	Sgt	18	RNZAF	04.09.40	N1628
REES, David Keith	RAF No. 748248	Sgt	n/k	RAF	20.02.41	N3446
REVILL, Harold	RAF No. 747795	LAC	n/k	RAF	28.05.40	L6953
ROBINSON, Ivan Norton	NZ40208	Sgt	20	RNZAF	22.07.41	T4071
SADAWA, Stanislaw	PAF No. 781291	Sgt	30	PAF	05.09.41	N1679
SANDERS, George Allan Paul	Can./ R.91798	Sgt	20	RCAF	18.03.42	N1629
SCOTT, Horace	RAF No.77368	P/O	33	RAF	28.05.40	L6959
SHARPE, Norman	RAF No. 67097	P/O	20	RAF	18.08.41	N1651
SHAW, Ian Garstin	RAF No. 40265	F/O	n/k	RAF	24.08.40	L7027
SKANDERA, Erwin	RAF No. 780711	Sgt	21	PAF	19.04.41	L6973
SLATTER, Dudley Malins	RAF No. 44597	P/O	26	RAF	19.07.40	L7016
SMITH, Roderick Giles	Can./ R.92555	Sgt	22	RCAF	11.04.42	N3503
SMITHSON, Richard	RAF No. 46174	Sgt	25	RAF	22.07.41	T4071
SNOOK, Alfred James	RAF No. 917338	Sgt	23	RAF	29.03.42	AA384
STORRIE, Alexander James	RAF No. 43641	F/O	24	RAF	20.11.40	N1626
TAYLOR, Peter John	RAF No. 958721	Sgt	20	RAF	15.05.41	T3955
TOOMBS, Frank Albert	RAF No. 79221	P/O	n/k	RAF	15.11.40	N1547
TOWNSEND, George Cherry	RAF No. 1305422	F/Sgt	n/k	RAF	15.01.42	N3422
TRAILL, Robert Alfred Edmund	RAF No. 36018	S/L	27	RAF	12.03.41	N3451
TRESSAM, Thomas Edward	Can./ R.75814	Sgt	25	RCAF	08.12.41	N1570
TURNER, Robert Charles	RAF No. 751362	Sgt	n/k	RAF	28.08.40	N1574
WALDEN, Gordon Fitzgerald	NZ402117	F/Sgt	26	RNZAF	26.02.42	T3995
WALLACE, Jack Fisher	NZ401735	Sgt	20	RNZAF	23.02.41	N3388
WATSON, Frederick Stanley	Can./ C.1372	F/L	26	RCAF	11.10.41	AA281
WESTOBY, Gerald Francis	RAF No. 1254338	Sgt	24	RAF	15.08.41	N1692
WHITEHOUSE, Edward Hammond	RAF No. 521432	F/L	24	RAF	28.05.40	L6959
WHITLEY, David	RAF No. 42036	P/O	21	RAF	28.08.40	N1574
WHIGHTMAN, David	RAF No. 903325	AC2	24	RAF	15.05.40	L6991
WILLIAMS, Dennis Conon	RAF No. 41230	F/O	n/k	RAF	04.04.41	T3913
WILLIAMS, Edward Vivian	RAF No. 746874	F/Sgt	21	RAF	04.11.41	T4053
WINTER, Ralph Henry John	RAF No. 1386870	Sgt	n/k	RAF	10.01.42	T3931
WISE, John Francis	RAF No. 746875	Sgt	n/k	RAF	19.08.40	L6983*
WOLF, Hiram	Can./ R.77476	Sgt	24	RCAF	01.01.42	N3432
WOOD, Albert Douglas	NZ401819	Sgt	24	RNZAF	08.04.41	N3424
WORLEDGE, George Edward	RAF No. 1376105	Sgt	26	RAF	04.03.41	N1794
YOUNG, Robert Bett Mirk	NZ40197	Sgt	22	RNZAF	08.10.40	N1627

*Baled out but aircraft returned safely to base.

Total : 139

Australia: 5, Canada: 11, Ireland (Eire): 1, Newfoudland: 1, New Zealand: 15, Poland: 8, United Kingdom: 98

n/k: not known

Boulton Paul Defiant Mk. I N1535
No. 264 Squadron
Squadron Leader Philip A. HUNTER
Kirton-in-Lindsey (UK), July-August 1940

Boulton Paul Defiant Mk. I N1801
No. 264 Squadron
Pilot Officer Frederick D. HUGHES
Biggin Hill (UK), March 1941

Boulton Paul Defiant Mk. I N3328
No. 151 Squadron
Wittering (UK), Spring 1941

Boulton Paul Defiant Mk. I V1110
No. 410 (RCAF) Squadron
Ayr (UK), January 1942

SQUADRONS! - The series

SQUADRONS!
No.54
Phil H. LISTEMANN
The Hawker
Biplane Fighters

AT WAR.
STUDY, HISTORY AND STATISTICS
No.137 Squadron
1941 - 1945
COMPILED BY
H. LISTEMANN
WITH
CHRIS THOMAS

USN AIRCRAFT
1922-1962
Vol.7:
Designation Letter
'F' (Pt-4)
NN

James Edgar JOHNSON DSO** DFC*

www.RAF-IN-COMBAT.com
- USN Aircraft 1922-1962 -
- Squadrons! -
- RAF, Dominion and Allied squadrons at War -
- Allied Wings -
- Fighter Leaders -
- Prints (Aces and Leaders) -

Fighter Leaders
of the RAF, RAAF, RCAF, RNZAF & SAAF in WWII
Volume VII
Phil H. Listemann

ALLIED WINGS
No.19
The English Electric CANBERRA
B(I).8
Phil H. LISTEMANN

SQUADRON
No.17
Phil H. LISTEMANN
The Curtiss
Mohawk

www.ingramcontent.com/pod-product-compliance
Lightning Source LLC
Chambersburg PA
CBHW041947140726
48006CB00002BA/266